STO

FRIENDS
OF ACPL

W9-BCB-388

3-30-72

GYPSY FIRES
IN AMERICA

*Gypsy ornaments like those
of Hindu nomads*

GYPSY FIRES
IN AMERICA

*A Narrative of Life Among the
Romanies of the United States
and Canada*

By
IRVING BROWN

*With Many Illustrations
from Photographs*

KENNIKAT PRESS
Port Washington, N. Y./London

GYPSY FIRES IN AMERICA

Copyright 1924 by Harper & Brothers
Reissued in 1972 by Kennikat Press by arrangemei
with Harper & Row, Publishers, Inc.
Library of Congress Catalog Card No: 70-159067
ISBN 0-8046-1660-4

Manufactured by Taylor Publishing Company   Dallas, Texas

1676715

CONTENTS

ILLUSTRATIONS

[vii]

ILLUSTRATIONS

GYPSY FIRES
IN AMERICA

GYPSY FIRES
IN AMERICA

CHAPTER I

WORLD WANDERERS

*Odd Encounters. Coppersmith and Nomad
Gypsies*

IT was early November, but more like the
warm, moist days of spring. In the distance,
the mist was a blur of azure, almost hiding the
hills. In the near-by hollows the vapor was a
golden sea, glowing with an inner light. It made
the smooth, silvery trunks of a glade of beech
trees seem so soft that the eye lingered in a long
caress. It dampened the grass, giving luster to
its greenness, and moistened the brown soil,
turned up by the fall plowing, enriching the air
with robust, life-giving odors. All day the sun
had warmed the earth. How good it felt on my
back as I swung along the country road! How
its ruddy rays flared through the mist, against a
clump of maples, lighting the leafy branches, like
tongues of crimson flame!

[1]

Nature, dressed like a gypsy, was indulging in a final fling of joy, before the dullness of winter had set in. A surge of life lingered in the atmosphere.

Cincinnati and the endless chain of duties had disappeared. I was hunting for gypsies. Something had told me I should find them. Was it merely because I had had a premature attack of spring fever, because I needed them, and had the will to believe? Or was it something in the blood, something in the wine-like air that whispered the message: The Romanies are here? Before I had become as one of them, I would spend weeks in fruitless search; but now some hidden impulse would usually take me to the camp. At times it was almost uncanny.

From where the road curved over the brow of a hill I caught a glimpse of several tents, with the blue smoke lazily rising and melting into the mist. My heart began to beat excitedly and my breath to come faster. I felt all the mingled joy and timidity of the lover. I wanted to run down the hill or shout; but instead, I stood there breathless, my feet lagging, as in a dream. It is a strange thrill, and one I never dared confess until I found how common it is among those who take an interest in the Romanies.

I noticed that they had autos, instead of wagons, but it did not mean that they were not true gypsies; and coming closer, I saw a group

[2]

of girls dressed with all the radiance of the autumn landscape—orange and green gowns, scarlet silk kerchiefs over their smooth black hair, and against their golden skins necklaces of gold coins glistening dully in comparison with the flashing teeth and eyes. They were Nomads, gypsies heart and soul, taking from modern industry only what fitted their age-old needs as wanderers. One of them called to me, as I passed, but I paid no particular attention, as I thought she merely wanted to tell my fortune. I approached the eldest of the men, a stout gypsy with high boots, a broad felt hat, and side whiskers. *"Sar mai san, kako?"* ("How are you, uncle?")

"Mišto. Sast'avesta," he replied. *"Katar aves, prala?"* ("Whence come you, brother?") *"Dikhlian amare Romen?"* ("Have you seen any of our people?")

I answered them, casually letting fall the information that I was part Romani. It had not been hard to convince myself of this; but all the non-gypsies to whom I have told it have simply been amused. As for brazenly telling it to a gypsy, it was so presumptuous—that it was believed.

Refusing a chair—the one and only in the camp—I half reclined on a heap of feather beds and cushions that had been aired and sunned since morning, and listened to the account of their

[3]

wanderings, which had covered half the earth.
They had recently come from Brazil by way of
Cuba. I had been in Cuba myself, the summer
before, and the first frost had brought nostalgic
visions of that "green isle in the sea," that vast
perfumed garden, clothed in tropical luxuriance
and bathed in shimmering light. These, and still
more enchanting visions of unknown lands, were
evoked as they talked of their travels.

Night had fallen. The fire burned low, letting
the chill November air and darkness fill the tent.
Somewhere in the distance a dog barked, breaking the silence. The hum of an auto was heard
down the road. The machine stopped and several
men got out. One of them came to the door of
the tent and began to talk in *Romanes*. The
voice was familiar. I had heard it only recently.
Yes, it was that of Spiro le Tsinasko, the ever-
smiling, ever-singing Spiro, whom I had seen a
few months before in a camp in Cuba. I jumped
up and hurried into the starlight. It was he,
almost as surprised to find me there as I had been
to hear his voice again, so unexpectedly.

We gathered together after supper in another
tent, in front of which a merry fire was crackling.
Bebe's wife, Butsiara, was nursing the baby.
Uncle Liubo was reclining against the pile of red
feather beds, a child nestling in either arm. The
older children, Todoro and Simziana, were lean-
ing forward, their eyes sparkling in the firelight,

as they eagerly listened to the song their father was singing, *"Le Rakli kai Barili ando Lulojai"* ("The Girl Who Grew Up in a Flower"). "A great song," as he explained, "more than five hundred years old."

The next, the *"Mesikanski Ghili,"* composed by Liubo and his family, dated back only a few years and commemorated the wanderings and tribulations of the tribe during the World War, when Mexico and the United States deported them each time they crossed the border.

Once Spiro began, he could sing from the setting sun till dawn. "Sing the one about Yanko's brother," the children pleaded. It was a veritable epic of the race; but not having a memory like Spiro, who could neither read nor write, and therefore carried it all in his head, I can only recall a fragment, which began:

> *"He Yanko! O Yanko!*
> *Lesko pral pandado."*

After telling of his imprisonment and the weeping of his brothers, it relates how the prisoner spent the dreary hours in jail, making music on a flute. So deep was his sorrow, and so perfectly did he express it in his melodies, that even the hardened heart of the jailer was stirred. "What beautiful music!" he exclaimed. "Where did you find such a marvelous flute?" Yanko's brother answered that he had made it from a twig of a

[5]

wonderful tree in the forest, under which he had lain one night. It was a musical tree, and as the wind swept through its leaves it sighed a soft lament: "Sister Wind! Sister Wind! Why must I always stay here? It is lonely. The birds, who taught me how to sing, have flown; the turtle dove that mourned so sweetly for its young, the nightingale that warbled to its mate. Oh, that I were free to follow you!" There must be some magic in that flute, thought the jailer; and he determined to get it. He offered the gypsy money, but the prisoner only shook his head. He wanted but one thing—his freedom, freedom to return to those he loved. Of what use was money to him in the jail?

Now the lovely music that floated from the cell ceased to give the jailer pleasure. It only reminded him that his efforts to gain possession of the instrument were useless. He was unable to sleep. He was unable to eat. At last he went to Yanko's brother and offered him his freedom in exchange for the marvelous flute. The gypsy gave it to him. The heavy door was unbolted, and with a cry of joy he ran out into the forest, like the wind—free. The jailer took the flute and tried to play on it; but it only gave out a harsh squeak, like the hinges of the prison door. What he held in his hands was merely a dry, hollow twig, for the soul of the flute was the

gypsy's soul. It had fled with Yanko's brother
—to freedom.

This was the song, as well as I can remember
it; but, alas! as I have said, I have not a memory
for songs like Spiro, nor could I catch all the
words, for as he sang them they sounded at times
like the cooing of doves, the notes of the nightingale, and then again like the sighing of the
wind.

"Did you compose these songs?" I asked
Spiro.

"Some," he answered, "have been handed down
from father to son for no one knows how long.
Others we make up on summer nights, when a lot
of us gather around the camp fire."

The conversation drifted to the question of
where they should spend the winter. Prospects
of making a living in Cincinnati were not very
bright. The year before a fellow gypsy had received a long jail sentence for *XoXano baro,* and
the authorities and the people were suspicious.
Prophesying was barred, and nothing allowed
save phrenology, since it was supposed to be
scientific. "Isaiah himself and other Old Testament prophets would have a hard time here," I
remarked.

"You mean Isaiah Stanley, the old English
Romaniček?" asked Liubo. *"Či drabarel.* He
doesn't tell fortunes. He peddles oilcloth."

Their money was getting low. They would

have to make some more in one way or another;
but the idea of spending the winter in a dingy
city did not appeal to them. Was not their freedom worth more than a crust of bread? Winter
was fast coming on; but it was not so much the
cold that urged them to be moving. Had not
Liubo's eldest son, Serga, been born in a tent in
western Ontario when the thermometer was
twenty below zero? What are icy blasts and
scorching tropical rays to the Children of the
Sun and Wind? Life was too tame here. They
were haunted by a feverish desire to go beyond
the walls of the horizon. Better times lay somewhere in the past or somewhere in the future. In
the meantime, there were golden memories and
roseate visions. Doubtless, on arriving at the
Land of Heart's Desire they would find it just
as dull, but no matter as long as nothing could
rob them of their illusions. They would cheat
the tedium of the present, with a laughter in their
children's eyes and the songs in their hearts.
They would dream of some promised land, as yet
unvisited.

As I listened to their animated discussion as to
whether they would follow the *patteran* westward to the setting sun, or southward to the
tropics, I shared their keen nostalgia for other
days, other lands, and other constellations rising
at the end of the long trail.

Close beside the tent was a tiny brook. I

*There is always laughter
in the children's eyes*

could hear its waters chuckling as though to say, "When everything is locked in chains of ice, we'll still be free, somewhere in the Gulf of Mexico, where porpoises are leaping in sheer delight, and redsnappers, darting in and out among the waving seaweed, are leaving wakes of silvery bubbles." The gypsies, too, must have heard this, for Mexico was the spot that they had decided on when I left.

Trudging homeward to the city, I passed a factory, its dusty windows giving out the ghastly artificial glow of mercury lamps. Hundreds of men were toiling there in the night shift, week in, week out, so that the machines should never be idle, machines more valuable than human happiness.

The next few days I was too busy to return to the camp. I had had just enough gypsying to make me long for more. The song of Yanko's brother kept going through my mind, making me regret I had not written it down. When I went back they had gone.

Perhaps I shall follow them to Mexico, though hunting for a particular gypsy is like hunting for the particular song sparrow that sang at your window last season. Perhaps I shall come across him by chance, in the pine groves of California, beside the Pacific, or under the flamboyant trees beside the Caribbean.

The sight of Spiro had made me appreciate

what is one of the greatest joys in a gypsy's life, the joy of unexpected meetings. We have so many *things* to occupy our minds that we often forget the great truth, which every gypsy knows —that nothing matters so much to human beings as other human beings, sweethearts, children, or friends. It is only in a great crisis that the truth is driven home to us, in parting or in death, when it is often too late.

I have had a number of odd encounters with gypsies, for the Romani world is a small one; but the following is one of the most curious and the most fortunate.

On returning to Barcelona, in the summer of 1922, I went at once to the gypsy café, Villa Rosa. Many of the former singers and dancers had gone, but I found one of the most interest‑ ing, Varia, the Russian Romani. She was drink‑ ing at a table with some wealthy Spaniards, whom she was entertaining with her lively con‑ versation and her hypnotic glances. Rising be‑ side her chair and clicking her heels on the floor in a passionate staccato, she lifted her arms above her head and held them poised a moment, while her hands suddenly curved, then seemed to float slowly upon the air. I can think of nothing equally graceful save, perhaps, the curling of a wisp of smoke. Did the gypsies learn this move‑ ment as they danced before the wreathing incense of some Hindu temple, or from the sinuous columns rising from a thousand camp fires?

The moment she noticed me there was a gleam of recognition. Without finishing the dance or waiting to get her "present" from the Spaniards, she came and sat down with me. All pretense of gayety was gone. With me, a Romani, she could be herself. Rapidly she told me that Dionisio, her *Rom,* was dead—Dionisio, the best dancer of Spain in his day, the man for whom she had run away from her parents as a young girl, telling the Petrograd police that they were trying to sell her as a prostitute, her father and mother, whom she loved above all else—save Dionisio. And now he was lying in the cold earth and she was alone.

The Gitanos she knew, whom she seemed to resemble so perfectly, were really an alien race, as much Spanish as Romani. Since her girlhood she had not heard the gypsy of her fathers, except as I had spoken it to her two years before. What had become of her parents and her sisters since the revolution in Russia? Would she ever see them again?

The next day was her birthday. I accepted her invitation to celebrate it quietly, and went to her room in the Calle San Ramón the following evening. The street was holding its yearly fiesta, and it was all I could do to force my way through the crowd. It was with something of a shock

[11]

that I found Varia dressed entirely in black,
having seen her the night before in a bright
Manila shawl. Her features were somewhat
haggard.

For three days she had not slept. The infant
son whom Dionisio had left her was ill. Each
morning, after the strain of trying to make
others gay all night in Villa Rosa, she had come
home and watched by the bedside of the child
until forced to go back to work.

The Catalonian woman who stayed in the
room while Varia was working was sent for cakes
and a bottle of *anis;* but the party was far from
gay. From time to time the baby would faintly
wail and Varia would rush to comfort him.
From below came the sound of a band playing
for the street festival, the faint noise of the
shuffling feet of hundreds of dancers on the pavement, and occasional shouts of joy—sounds that
seemed ironical and jeering.

For the first time since the death of Dionisio,
Varia had found some one to whom she could
confess all her grief, her present troubles, and her
anxiety for the future. Knowing the relief which
expression of her sorrows would bring her, I did
not have the heart to change the subject. Worst
of all was the fear of losing her place. The
patrons of the café liked to see new faces among
the dancers. The pay from the proprietor was
almost nothing. Her earnings were chiefly in

tips from wealthy patrons, large at times and at others negligible. Who would give money to a girl whose eyes were red from weeping or whose heart was heavy? Besides, there was no telling how long the café itself might last. And then what? As for herself, nothing mattered much now—but the baby? Dionisio had made and squandered huge sums with gypsy recklessness, little thinking that almost at the moment he was to disappear from the world a second self would enter it, helpless, dependent, at once a consolation and a problem. Tenderly she held the little boy in her arms. All the deep gypsy love of wife and mother was concentrated in the child, whose future was so uncertain. He was better now, sleeping restfully, as she laid him once more on the bed. Varia was free to go out for a brief change, before going back to her task of amusing others in the stuffy café. Instinctively, she thought of the sea, as though its infinite waters might wash away her troubles, and its cosmic greatness be like a healing glimpse of the everlasting arms that are always underneath. What would become of her? How could she ever reach her family again?

Three weeks later I was sitting in the smoking room of the *France* bound for New York. A warm discussion was going on between a restaurant owner, an international journalist, and myself. Of a sudden my companions had turned to stare at some one who had just entered. It was a black-haired girl in a bright-colored gown, walking across the room. Not the rich rose-magenta of the dress, nor the full, sinuous, elastic figure it revealed, nor the dark features of the girl, which were irregular but impelling, nor the walk, as graceful and beautiful as a panther's, was the cause of every eye being focused upon her. It was the strange something, the mysterious magic, the unknown quantity, which is the chief ingredient of beauty, which fascinated us. The former discussion was totally forgotten, and an instant later, when the conversation was resumed, it turned unconsciously on beautiful women. The elderly restaurant owner began to recount his amorous exploits.

That afternoon the journalist came to me and said, "For the first time in my life I envy erudition."

"How is that?"

"You can speak gypsy. The girl we saw this morning in the smoking room is a Romani. She is with the Russian troupe."

I inquired of a member of the company, which was coming from Paris to give artistic tableaux with singing and dancing in one of the principal theaters of New York. He pointed her out to me, sitting in a steamer chair, in a corner of the hurricane deck, where she had kept by herself during the entire trip.

I spoke to her in gypsy. She talked it fluently and we chatted for a while in the language. She was lonely, lonely as only a Romani who is separated from her race and her family can be lonely. Day after day she had sat there, gazing over the blue depths and finding consolation in their very solitude and vastness.

Learning that she had once lived in Petrograd, I asked her if she happened to have heard of a girl named Varia, who had run away in that city with a Spanish dancer. She stared tensely for a moment before answering, "She is my sister."

To make certain I asked her to tell the month of Varia's birthday, and other details, which she gave correctly.

The parents had long since forgiven the daughter's flight, and with the true gypsy love for their children they longed for her.

"Where did you see her? If I only knew her address!" When I gave it to her she leaped from her chair in delight. "I shall write the moment I land." If the sister's joy was great, what must Varia's have been on receiving the letter!

There are countries where a larger percentage of the population is gypsy, such as Bulgaria, Serbia, and Rumania; but none contains as many varied types of true Romanies as America. The reason for this is obvious. The United States, having attracted immigrants from more

different lands than any other country, it would
have been strange if it had not also attracted the
least settled element in those countries — the
gypsies. Naturally it appealed to the most
nomadic of them, the most gypsy, as nomadism
is their central trait, which has largely determined their occupations, customs, beliefs, and
even their physical characteristics.

The New World is the land of the restless, the
paradise of those who refuse to stay put. Nowhere do the gypsies thrive as here. They need
a country which is not too settled, so that they
may camp where they please, and one which is
not too thinly inhabited or too poor, since they
depend on the prosperity of others for their support.

Old records show that they came here, mostly
deported from England, in Colonial days. A
large group was also sent from France to Biloxi,
Mississippi. But by far the majority are recent
arrivals. Of the thousands I have questioned in
this country, most of those over forty were foreign born. This year I met a *Romaničel,* a
Boswell, born in New York State in 1857, who
claimed that his father was among the first to
leave England. The English gypsies were the
first to come here in any considerable numbers.

It is customary to speak of Spanish gypsies,
English gypsies, Hungarian gypsies, and so on
indefinitely, though no gypsy scholar seriously

The Romanies doubtless came from India at various times, and from slightly different tribes; but the typical gypsy is Hindu in appearance as well as in language

questions the fact that they are a single race with a common origin — India. After entering Europe toward the end of the Middle Ages, the majority, after spreading throughout the entire continent, gradually began to restrict their wanderings to certain groups of countries, certain countries, or even certain districts, not to mention the fact that many have even settled down.

For that reason it is customary to speak, not only of English gypsies, for example, but to further differentiate—the Devonshire Stanleys, the New Forest Smiths, or the Derbyshire Boswells. The same is true of Spain, for instance, where the Romanies themselves speak of Estremaduran, Andalusian, or Catalonian gypsies. The same thing has happened in America. There is a tribe of Boswells who, for many years, wandered almost exclusively on the Pacific coast; another whose beat is the Middle West; and a third who traveled only between western Ontario and Nova Scotia. A certain Wells family oscillates between a camping ground not far from Jersey City, and another near Baltimore, while another group makes a circuit of Iowa, Illinois, and Wisconsin. So regular are the movements of this latter family that there is scarcely a day in the year that I could not say they are in such and such a spot.

Even in the United States, the majority of Romanies live in houses part of the time, and a few have settled down completely. Some two hundred Hungarian gypsies, for instance, have purchased a solid block in a Pennsylvania city, where they have lived for years.

In America there are gypsies from every portion of Europe, and a few from Asia. The only Spanish gypsies I have ever met on the American continent were in Cuba. The presence of Portuguese gypsies has not been reported outside of Brazil. But I have spoken with Rumanian, Russian, Serbian, Bulgarian, Greek, Turkish, Hungarian, German, English, and Scotch Romanies.

The majority of gypsies in the United States, however, escape any such strict classification. One can only call them Nomads, or simply gypsies. Many of them came to this country from Serbia in the 'nineties, when stringent laws were passed against wandering in that country; but they can scarcely be called Serbian, since their immediate ancestors traveled from Bosnia to Russia by way of Transylvania, Galicia, and Poland; and more remote forbears had roamed for generations in Rumania.

There is scarcely a family of them one meets to-day, in the United States, which has not been in half a dozen countries, principally those of South America, but in some cases even Japan and Australia. One group I met had been in Calcutta, where the chief was struck by the similarity of their tongue to that of the natives.

They live almost exclusively by the fortune-
telling of the women. The men traded horses
to some extent until a few years ago, but dealing
in horses was not a regular profession among
them as among the English gypsies in this country. To-day they travel by either train or auto—
mobilensa; and recently a Nomad gave his profession to the police as auto dealer. Many are
prosperous; but once a considerable sum has been
accumulated, it is usually spent with reckless disregard for the future.

The automobile has not succeeded in robbing
them of their picturesqueness. They still remain
the shyest, most nomadic, and most colorful of
any body of gypsies in the entire world. Less
has been written about them than about the
others, because in their constant wanderings they
have remained aloof and elusive.

As for their own name for themselves, the most
general is *Kalo Rom,* or Black Gypsy. They are
further known by family or tribal names—
Mačvano, Kalderaš, Budisare, Maritsare, or
Karavlasi, for instance.

It would be almost as difficult to gauge their
numbers in the United States as to count the
swallows, but some idea may be obtained from
the fact that last Christmas there were three
hundred families of them in the neighborhood of
Chicago alone. At a gathering for a wedding
near San Francisco the police estimated over a

thousand. At a rough guess, I should say there
were about fifty thousand of the Nomads in the
United States and Canada, and fifty thousand of
the other varieties all told.

The gypsies most closely allied to the Nomads
in language, dress, and customs, are the Coppersmiths. The latter are likewise far-wandering,
and scarcely to be associated with any one country; but their trade has brought them into closer
contact with the *Gaje,* and has made them more
industrious. They are wild and primitive, but
have less of the care-free joy of living than the
Nomads. Relatively few bands of them are to be
found in this country.

There is no difficulty in recognizing the
Nomad and Coppersmith women by their appearance—red-silk kerchiefs over their heads,
dresses of many gay colors, and necklaces of
large gold coins.

Names, however, tell nothing, as in talking to
Gentiles they always give wh'at they call their
nav gajikanes, or names in Gentile style. Sometimes it is a mere translation of an East Euro-
pean name into English. Ivan Stefanovitch be-
comes John Stevenson. The numerous tribe of
Mitchells descends from a patriarch by the name
of MiXail. The *nav Romanes,* or name in gypsy
style, is formed by adding the father's given
name to that of the son, Tsino's George, O
Giorgi le Tsinasko, or O Liubo le Eframos. The

Although the Nomads often live in houses during the winter, they always camp in summer

Gajikanes names of the women, being taken from men's first names, are sometimes amusing. About half the fortune tellers' licenses are issued to Mary John. Occasionally you find one such as Millie Mike or Rosie Pete.

The various varieties of gypsy seldom mix, although they side with one another against the *Gajo*. The English gypsies especially are inclined to regard the Nomads and other Romanies with a certain hostility, referring to them as "them bloody Turks," or "the Bear Folki," declaring that they have "spoiled" the country. The Nomads say the same of the *XoroXane Rome,* the Turkish gypsies in America, accusing them of various crimes.

An English *Romaničel* told me that one day some Nomads, whom he spoke of as "Turks," asked him in gypsy if he were a Romani. "No, I'm not," he answered, naïvely. It was only when the "Turks" began to laugh that he realized that he had given himself away.

The more primitive and barbaric varieties are friendlier with the others; and as they all become acquainted, they tend to reunite.

After these general considerations of the various kinds of Romanies to be met with in North America, let me give you a description of a tribe of Coppersmith gypsies found here. The most picturesque sight I think I have ever seen was in

[21]

the city which is usually considered the most prosaic—the city of pork and grime—Chicago. A band of Coppersmiths had installed themselves in a large vacant yard, in the district of the junk dealers, near Lake Street, within sight of the tired suburbanites on the elevated. As I entered the inclosure, the men were at work, dressed in fantastic garb. In appearance they were like the typical Hindu, with full, wavy beards, and long black locks that fell on their shoulders. Some had Russian smocks, others red-silk shirts, with innumerable plaits, and, instead of coats, a sort of vest, with large silver buttons. Their trousers were voluminous, and stuffed into high leather boots. The dress of the women was no less brilliant in coloring. One of them, with a headdress made from a scarlet kerchief, from which silver coins dangled, and a necklace of ancient gold medals, came forward, on seeing me, and taking me for an easy prey, a *Gajo,* she began to beg: "Give money to buy bread. My children— hungry."

"Daia," I answered, in gypsy, scrutinizing one of the coins, an eighteenth-century Spanish piece —"Mother, when you go begging, it's against the rule to wear a small fortune where every *Gajo* can see it." Her expression changed from blank amazement to delight. *"Rom san tu!"* ("You are a gypsy!") she exclaimed—and invited me to stay to dinner, which proved a sump-

[22]

tuous meal, as gypsy meals go, served on a silver tray.

The anvils at which the men were working were of a form as old as the Iron Age. They were made with a base that could be driven into the ground, so that any chance field might be changed to a smithy. The hammers and bellows, too, were of their own age-old pattern. A hollow in the ground was their forge, and in it an enormous copper vat was taking on wondrous tints of purple, red, and green, under the heat. Though their tools were primitive, they were working on a job which no one in Chicago was willing to attempt, according to the man for whom it was being done, a manufacturer, who was there watching them, and urging them to hurry, as part of his large plant was being held up until it was done. At night, particularly, it was fascinating to watch them work, in the glare of the flaming forge, with Rembrandtesque effect of light and shade.

They had traveled over all Europe, and had made a great deal of money. Even the young boys could speak five or six languages, imperfectly but fluently. I found a newspaper article on these same gypsies. It told that when they first landed in the United States the immigration authorities, looking askance at their lack of baggage, except for what they had tied up in quilts, were going to deport them as paupers, until they showed thousands of dollars in gold; whereupon they decided to deport them as undesirables, thinking that such a quantity of money must have been stolen.

In Chicago they were camping in a house. But quite in the traditional style, with no furnishings but feather beds and cushions, and a table with legs sawed off within a foot of the ground. They squatted on the floor, around a wide silver eating tray, on which all the food was placed. As in the Orient and at picnics, fingers were the chief tableware. In one corner, however, was a handsome samovar of antique form, and on the walls were drapes of gayly colored cloth.

A few years later I found a type of gypsy which forms a link between the Nomads and the Coppersmiths. I was walking down Mott Street in New York, where Little Naples blends with Little Canton or Shanghai, looking for local color, when just in front of me I spied the gay garments of a gypsy woman. I followed her into a hallway and saw her disappear through a door in the rear. I entered without knocking, for, whether because of their custom of living in tents, or whether because they are like one big family, a true gypsy seldom does. A knock at the door, the ring of the bell, usually means a policeman, a truant officer, or some other interfering *Gajo,* and prepares for a poor welcome.

The typical Coppersmith anvil is driven into the ground. The gypsies are skilled handicraftsmen

The room was bare, except for the heap of red feather beds in one corner, an ikon in another, and a stove in the center, on which a huge kettle was bubbling, giving out a savory odor of chicken, rice, peppers, and herbs. The woman was alone, but soon the others returned for dinner—meal hours are whenever anyone feels like preparing anything. The *khaini* was done. A huge round tray of hammered copper was placed on the floor, with pieces of bread. There were eight or nine of us, and only two plates, three spoons, and one fork. The kettle was placed on the tray and each one helped himself and ate with his fingers. The method was messy, but the chicken excellent.

A gallon jug of red wine was brought from a neighboring *Italianitso birto*. Raising his glass in the direction of the ikon, one of the Romanies made the sign of the cross. *"Kames mol?"* ("Do you like wine?") the father asked one of the girls, a radiant creature with an expression that any actress would have envied.

"Me čumidavle!" ("I kiss it!") she cried.

From time to time other gypsies dropped in and joined the circle around the tray. The wide world over, in all ranks of society, there are few pleasures as enjoyable as a dinner party; but with most of us they are elaborate affairs that we half dread because of the trouble they involve in advance. Not so with the gypsies. "Take pot

[25]

luck," is not a mere phrase. Scarcely a meal is eaten among the Coppersmiths or Nomads, but what there are guests. And the best of breaking bread together is that it is one of the few pleasures that never pall.

A melon from a pushcart at the door furnished the dessert. As the smiling mother divided it, with a wicked-looking clasp-knife, which she took from her bosom, she kissed each piece. *"Gugli"* ("It is sweet"), she said, handing them to us. Sweet it was indeed, sweet with Romani kindness.

After dinner, Uncle Yanši told a wonder tale. He was an elderly gypsy, with bare feet and legs protruding from wide linen trousers, as wide as skirts. This part of his costume was, like his name, Hungarian, but his shirt was a genuine gypsy *gad,* with wide orange and green plaits, and a large whirligig pattern. Yanši was capable of making a good living, as either a musician or a coppersmith, but preferred to let his wife support him by telling fortunes. His real calling was that of a teller of tales. Such marvels as he could relate: giant birds that carried men on their backs to far-off lands, and told them of dazzling treasures! To him, as to the little children that listened open-eyed, the miracles of man that rose about them in the city, where humanity has triumphed over nature, were either uninteresting, mere things, lifeless and dull, or unbelievable. And sometimes I wonder myself if there is not more human truth in a fairy tale than in a statistical chart. Both are symbolic.

In the course of the conversation, I was asked if I was not married; and considerable surprise was expressed when I replied in the negative. "How do you live, then?" I told them I was a professor, which in certain classes of society invariably means a male fortune teller, a runner of a "mit joint." Asked by a gypsy girl, Rosa, to display my talent, I answered that I could not tell a true fortune for less than five dollars—in advance. I thought I could get out of it in that manner. But, to my surprise, she put a five-dollar bill in my hand and held out her own for a reading. There was nothing to do but to go ahead. I pocketed the five dollars and took the hand, a beautiful hand, with long tapering fingers and rosy palms, the hand of an artist and a high-spirited young creature, pulsing with life. "Am I married?" she asked. Guessing from the question that she was not, I replied, "No." "Have I ever been?" As she was fully twenty, I knew it was safe to say, "Yes." Having been successful as to past and present, it was easy to tell the future, at least without fear of contradiction —for the moment. I made several safe predictions, one of which was that she would marry again soon. She was too attractive to remain a widow for long.

[27]

When I had finished, she offered to tell mine. "Put a piece of silver in my hand," she insisted. I gave her a quarter, expecting she would insist on more, but she did not. Her game was something else. After reading my thoughts, which I was having difficulty in concealing, she promised to say a charm which would bring me happiness. Mumbling some meaningless words, she took my hand in both hers and held it first to the left side of her bosom so that I could feel her heart beat, and then to the right. Next she held it to the left and right side of her waist. The performance was repeated on myself in the same four places, with our joined hands. She doubtless could have felt that my own heart was beating at a somewhat exhilarated rate. A few minutes later, when I put my hand in my vest pocket to give her back the five dollars she had given me, I found that she had spared me the pains, and had also saved me the trouble of getting rid of a few bills that were in my other vest pockets. She laughed when I discovered the loss, and returned me the money. "You are fairly good at *drabarimus* (fortune telling)," she said, "but I am much better." I was forced to agree.

"*Daia!*" ("Mother!") called a little girl of two, who already was a miniature of the mother, with shreds of red silk braided into her black tresses, with her seductive smile and her flashing eyes, born to fascinate. Observing the admiration in my glance, Rosa told me the story of the child. "She was born soon after my husband died," she said. "I was in camp with my father's people, and had gone a quarter of a mile from the tent to get some water. I was bending down by the spring, when all at once I heard a cry and there was the baby lying on the grass. I had been carrying some string and a pair of scissors with me and knew just what to do—the *purya* (the old women) tell us. And then I picked it up and carried it in my apron back to camp, laughing.

"When I got there the *purya* made me lie down. Some *Gaje* came along and asked my father what was the matter. He told them and they said he must get a doctor. 'What for?' my father asked. 'Maybe she'll die if you don't,' they said. So he sent for a doctor. When he came, he just touched me on the shoulder and said, 'Five dollars, please.'"

After chatting a while longer, Yanši finally said: "I must get to work. Are you coming with me?" I followed him to a garage where he kept his *mobile*. I got in beside him, and we set out through the East Side in his Packard to collect copper kettles and pans to mend.

"Why aren't you married?" Yanši asked me, point blank.

"I haven't enough money," I answered.

"That needn't worry you. My daughter Rosa

is a widow and has a child. She is twenty-two already. You see, I am telling you the truth. You can have her cheap—four hundred dollars." As I did not answer at once, he proceeded to enumerate her good qualities. "She can tell fortunes and *čorel misto;* she steals well, as you have seen. If you work, too, you will make plenty of money; but if you don't like to, she will support you. You are a *Rom* and you know how it is with us."

I have frequently been asked if the gypsy race is not dying out; and I have heard both gypsies and *Gaje* claim that it is. But in spite of decay and changes here and there, it is my belief that the race as a whole is not on the decline. They are perhaps the one primitive people whom contact with civilization has failed to exterminate. Love of children, love between the sexes, confined though it is by strict custom, and what amounts, among the Nomads, to the virtual selling of wives, and love among members of the race, combined with splendid health and stamina, keep them going. Their lives are a constant struggle that keeps them fit.

Perhaps, after our lightning-like civilization has burned itself out, the gypsy caravans will wind their way past crumbling skeletons of towering buildings. The gypsy, following the ever westward march of man, will then return to his

*Handsome samovars and silver cups are frequent
possessions of the Nomads and Coppersmiths; but
they count their children as their chief riches*

native land, unchanged.   The poet's prophecy
will be fulfilled:

"Only the hearthstone of old India
Will end the endless march of gypsy feet."

CHAPTER II

LOVE AMONG THE GYPSIES

IN all that relates to love the gypsies are both unusually bound by custom and unusually free. That this is an apparent paradox only guarantees its truth, for man is so balanced that he is a living paradox. Human tendencies are not like algebraic quantities. A minus y negates a plus y, but the fact one has a left arm does not prevent one from having a right arm.

The restrictions which the Romanies put on sex relations are like the jetties and levees raised beside a river to keep it from overflowing, and which have the effect of causing the current to flow more deeply and more swiftly.

By nature the gypsies are extremely passionate. They are a Southern race, with all the rapidly unfolding luxuriance of the tropics. Their senses are keen and their emotions have not been intellectualized. One has only to glance at a Romani girl to see how pure and strong the vital instinct flows in her blood: something in the sensuous, unfettered walk, something in the glitter of the eye, something in her whole feline being. One thinks at once of a flamboyant tree with its great scarlet flowers, or a graceful palm tree seen by lightning in the rush of a Cuban hurricane.

The gypsies are well aware of this appeal, and make capital of it, both as dancers and as fortune tellers. If women often go to them to have their hands read because of some heart interest, men frequently do the same because of a temporary heart interest in the gypsy girl herself. The aristocrats of Spain and Russia are not the only persons who have been swayed by the soft witchery of Romani girls. Many a lonely woodsman has returned from the North, to a men's lodging house in West Madison Street, Chicago, with a roll of bills, and has parted with a large portion of his money for the privilege of having some pretty *čei* hold his calloused hand.

As the gypsies have no taboo on words, sex matters are discussed with the utmost frankness, and morbid curiosity, sex phobias, and complexes are practically unknown. This lack of suppression, coupled with the fact that they use their lure to further their own interests, has given rise to the erroneous impression that they are unchaste. It is a curious fact that a Romani girl, for whom no phrase would have any terrors and who would think nothing of dancing a lascivious dance, would show a certain shyness before strange men of her own race. Her modesty is not a matter

[33]

of "keeping up appearances," but an inner bloom.

Nevertheless, there are flood times when the levees break. There are times when the power of passion sweeps aside the age-old laws which sway the Romani mind. And although they take more effective measures than other races that this shall not happen, when once it does, they show themselves more tolerant. However, in former times banishment from the tribe, and ceremonies of degradation and even mutilation, were sometimes resorted to, and are not wholly dead to-day.

Marriage frequently takes place soon after puberty, as in India, but with this difference: it is real, not merely another name for childhood betrothal. Until then the girls are under the strictest chaperonage. Love making goes on under the eyes of the parents. It is frank and open, something to be gloried in, not mocked at and secreted. It is not to be wondered at, therefore, that the race has kept itself remarkably pure and that sex relations outside of openly recognized unions are rarer than in *Gajo* society. Only thus could a handful of people have wandered over the broad face of the earth, continually among aliens, and have maintained its integrity.

The race has remained true to type also because of its aversions to mixed marriages. "It was against the gypsy religion," Johnston Boswell once said to me, "to marry a *Gajo*." Any number of instances might be cited to prove this point. And although this law is violated more and more frequently among the less wandering gypsies, such as the Anglo - American and Spanish, it is still preserved among the Nomads, in spite of an occasional pair of blue eyes to bear witness to a forbidden romance sometime in the past. **1676715**

One of the rare exceptions I have observed was that of a Coppersmith Romani who had married a Mexican Indian. It was at a large camp on the edge of Brooklyn. Noticing a girl in splendid gypsy attire, including the crimson silk kerchief over her head, who was squatting on the floor of a tent in the midst of a number of women who were speaking Spanish to her instead of *Romanes,* I was puzzled until I learned that she was a *Gaji* whom one of the men who had just returned from Mexico had recently married. The hair and features of the Indian girl were not unlike those of a Romani, and her mode of life had not been sufficiently different to make it difficult to adapt herself to the new ways. But it was obvious that the gypsy women who were instructing her in her duties considered her as an intruder.

Although there is much to be said for early marriages, the extreme youth of many gypsy parents may be one of the reasons why the race has never grown up. Recent biological investigations tend to show that children resemble their parents at the period of procreation: that the offspring of a young and vigorous couple are more apt to be stronger and more vigorous than the children of an elderly couple, and that the offspring of the latter will be more intellectual. Be it as it may, old and young not only dress alike but act alike, and are true companions. Show me a gypsy, whatever be his age, who has lost the buoyancy of youth. This lack of maturity is a barrier to their "progress," perhaps, but it is also the source of one of their chief charms.

Living together from early years gives a sense of comradeship to gypsy couples to an extent rarely seen among other peoples. And although friendship alone is not sufficient for a happy marriage, it forms a firm base, without which no union can be successful. Natural frankness and the adaptability of youth make most gypsy marriages a thing of permanence and beauty.

In the movies the husbands are often depicted as beating their wives. I have known isolated cases of this among the Spanish gypsies and some others, but none among the Nomads, except for a certain amount of good-natured give and take in a spirit of fun.

I have observed a case of husband beating, however, among the Anglo-American Romanies. A band of them were encamped in a country lane near Madison, Wisconsin, a few years ago. It was a beautiful July morning, and as I was walking along under the sun-drenched elms in the direction of the camp I came on the strange sight of a stocky, middle-aged gypsy walking down the road and weeping. His first name was Sampson, and although he was not the one whose wife's name was Delilah, his spouse had pulled out a handful of his hair and had punched his jaw. Instead of retaliating he was on his way to the *pien-tan,* or crossroads saloon, to seek consolation in *tato-pani.* When we returned to the tent the dishes were just as they had been left at breakfast. And no wife. A day passed, and nothing was seen of her. As the rest of the gypsies did not seem worried, I asked for an explanation, and was told that it was a regular occurrence for Sampson to get drunk and his wife to beat him. After doing so she invariably took the first train to her relatives, where she stayed until her husband begged her to come back to him.

Although gypsy wives and husbands are generally faithful to each other, gypsy marriages are not necessarily permanent. The fact that most Romani unions are happy makes divorce fairly uncommon; but in case the couples find themselves ill-assorted, separation is comparatively easy. There is none of the complicated machinery of divorce one finds in *Gajo* society. It is simply a case of mutual consent, or of arbitration before a council of the tribe.

[37]

Occasionally the proceedings are even simpler
—one or the other runs away. Complications,
however, are bound to arise; and running away,
while treated with frankness and a certain toler-
ance, is distinctly frowned upon. Snce the husband regards the money made by his wife as his
own, he usually deserts with the family ex-
chequer; and as the wife considers it hers, because
of earning it, she does the same. Naturally this
leads to trouble in either case, and of late even
to a monstrous breach of Romani custom—an
appeal to the American courts.

The moment this last method is resorted to,
there is literally no end to the trouble for everyone connected, even remotely, with the persons
concerned. In their own *kris,* or tribunal, the
gypsies tell the truth to one another, but the
moment they testify to the *Gaje* the old habits of
mendacity assert themselves, and the judge and
jury are confronted with a thousand conflicting
statements and hundreds of angry relatives.

Some time ago I attended such a trial at the
Stockyards Police Court, in the company of the
former chief, Ioano Adamovič, widely known as
"Joe Adams, the king of the gypsies." The
room was overflowing with Nomads in picturesque costume. Everyone was trying to talk
at once. The magistrate's gavel pounded continually on the desk, and the bluecoats were having their hands full trying to keep order among

the spectators. It was only the prestige of the former ruler that enabled us to get a place at all.

It was charged that "Princess" Mary had eloped not only with another tribesman, but also with the strong box belonging to her husband. On the witness stand she claimed that she had not left her husband, but had simply gone on a visit; and later she maintained that she had deserted him because of ill treatment, that she had not touched the money; and later that she had taken it and given it to her husband's own brothers, who had threatened to kill her if she did not; and later still that she had carried the money off because it was hers. Whatever else she may have stated, I do not know, for I finally grew tired of standing, and left in search of Joe Adams, who had already disappeared.

It would have been easy enough for the judge to detect the lies from the truth if the husband had not varied his charges even more widely and if the witnesses had not lied as stoutly under the cross-examinations of the magistrate and the counsel for the defense. When it suited their purpose they affirmed that they did not understand, and called for an interpreter or maintained a stolid silence. A moment later they would break out in a torrent of broken English that was fairly overwhelming. I was told that in the end the magistrate threatened them all with arrest for perjury, but on second thought, dismayed, no doubt, at the idea of a series of similar trials, he threw the case out of court.

Another complication arising from cases of *romni-našli,* or runaway wife, is the question of paying back the sum of money paid by the groom's father to that of the bride. An interesting case of this sort occurred not long ago among a band of Nomads who for many years had traveled in Canada. The affair was mentioned in the Montreal newspapers when it was taken to the courts, but, as usual, the truth of the matter was not arrived at in the *Gajo* tribunals. It was only from another gypsy, whom I found in a camp near Hamilton, Ontario, and from a relative of the girl, whom I met in Chicago, that I learned the actual details. In spite of the publicity already given the matter, it is better, perhaps, that I change the names of the principals.

In the summer of 1918 two Romani bands, those of Marko and Petri, were camping at a place about forty miles from Saskatoon in western Canada. Petri's daughter, Persa, was a girl of fifteen and the pride of the entire camp. Each of the boys of marriageable age paid court to her, but none was treated with preference.

Frequent visits were paid by the old chief, Marko, and his son, Milano, a handsome fellow of thirty, with somewhat aquiline features and the quick, restless gaze of a hawk. They were always received with considerable cordiality, as

Marko was well-to-do for a gypsy, and had been
a man of great influence among the Nomads of
all North America, whom he had tried to bring
into a closer union, of which he himself, of course,
was to have been the "King of Kings." He
failed, however, owing to the fact that he did not
enjoy the confidence of his fellow Romanies, and,
being a proud man, he retired with his tribe of
relatives to the remoter parts of Canada, where
he seldom came in contact with other clans.

He was pointed out to me once in the streets
of Vancouver, a good many years ago, before I
could speak his language or mingle with his
people. I saw him for only a moment, but I shall
never forget his commanding figure. He was
middle-aged then, but tall and stout and erect,
with flowing hair and side whiskers that formed
a sort of mane. His voice was deep and imperious, his lips full and smiling, with a smile of
triumph. People turned and stared at him—
especially the women.

During his visits to Petri he kept his eyes continually on Persa, and finally in due form he proposed that the girl should marry his son, Milano.
"Khate štar šela lire ande vast" ("Here is two
thousand dollars in your hand"), said Marko,
one day, taking from inside his shirt a roll of
Canadian bills, which was to serve as an in-
demnity for the loss of the daughter. Petri
allowed him to proceed to count it out for the

mere pleasure of feasting his eyes on the money. After some reflection he pushed it back to the owner, declaring that the match was impossible. "Let Milano marry a widow, a *pivli,* as he is a *pivlo* and much too old for Persa." A sardonic laugh must have gathered in Marko's heart, but he restrained it and made an effort to persuade the reluctant father.

"An older man is better for your daughter. You know the Romani saying: *'Terni romni dikhel pale'* ('A young wife is always looking about'). She needs some one strong and experienced to guide her, to hold her to her duty, and keep her looking straight ahead."

Persa was consulted by her father, and as the reserved attentions of a man of thirty were more flattering than the frank admiration of the boys her own age, of which she had become somewhat surfeited, she admitted that she was not indifferent to Milano. Still the father hesitated. There was something about the proposal he did not like. Marko had been too eager and too much in a hurry.

At last, however, he gave in to insistent demands, veiled threats, and offers of more money. Petri was anxious to visit friends and relatives in Nova Scotia and needed ready cash for the trip. The wedding was celebrated in the old style, without priest or marriage license, and with three days' merrymaking. In his cups Marko never took his eyes from the bride and continually called upon her to dance. He himself did a number of steps with considerable agility, in spite of his age.

After the ceremony Petri and his tribe broke camp and moved East.

Contrary to custom, the newly wedded couple were not given a tent of their own, but were obliged to live with the chief, who kept them constantly in sight and informed the bride that, owing to her tender years, her husband would refrain from asserting his conjugal rights for some time.

The attraction which Persa had felt for Milano gradually dwindled as she came to know him better and observed in him a smoldering vindictiveness that sought an outlet against those whom he felt were weaker than himself. Also her pride had been hurt by the fact that he had made no effort to really make her his own. Finally, resentment and distrust completely killed the faint love she had once felt.

Meanwhile Milano, who had felt no affection at first, began to be captivated by the beauty of the girl, the constant proximity, and the thought that she was his wife. Piqued by her growing coolness, his love rapidly grew, as a prairie fire is fanned to mighty conflagration by the north wind.

It was Marko who had originally been captivated by the girl, and, knowing her father would never allow her to marry him, had planned that his son should nominally wed her, and then divorce her, which would give him an opportunity of marrying her himself. Just before the time set for the separation, Milano proposed to Persa that they secretly leave the tribe. The girl was not a gypsy and a fortune teller for nothing. Reading the amorous glances of the father and son, and the looks of hate that they were exchanging more and more frequently, she saw in what quarter the storm was gathering, and laid her plans accordingly.

She knew that if she fled with Milano she was lost. Marko had already suggested a divorce on the pretext that the couple were not happy together—which was obviously the truth. There was no time to spare. She must act quickly. Her parents were by this time in Nova Scotia, across the continent. The members of the clan among whom she was now living would at least remain neutral. There was no hope through appealing to them. There remained but one chance—a desperate one. Not far off was a detachment of Northwest Mounted Police. They were hereditary enemies, but she knew from the experience of various gypsies that they were not to be corrupted like the police of the cities, and that they had a certain sense of chivalry.

Rising from her bed at night when all were

asleep, she slipped out of the tent and walked to the post. It was not without fear that she presented her case to the lieutenant on duty—embroidering on the story no doubt—but she found the gray-haired officer extremely sympathetic. In the morning a squad of police summoned the father and son, and a court was held. No crime had been committed and there was no precedent for the proceedings, but justice was delivered without the usual delays. The lieutenant declared that there never had been a marriage and that the girl was free to go where she pleased without restraint.

Easily said. But where was she going to get the money to rejoin her parents and how could the police prevent her from being detained by Marko, once she was at a safe distance from the officers? A fox knows many things, but a gypsy girl more, to paraphrase a Romani saying. Persa remained at the post for a few days, during which time she told the fortunes of all the troop—in spite of the fact that it was against the law—and raised enough cash, together with gifts from various kind-hearted people, to pay her fare to Nova Scotia, where she hoped to find her parents.

Several days had been lost in this manner before she was able to set out. She knew that her father-in-law and husband would attempt to head her off, but she kept her own counsel. The less

the *Gaje* had to do with the affair the better.
Before setting out she inquired in detail about all
the possible routes, the various junctions, and the
general direction of the principal towns on her
route. It was hardly necessary, however, as the
gypsies never forget a road they have once
traveled. She had made the trip once before by
rail with her parents, when she was a child.

There are three possible lines from Saskatoon,
all of which converge at a junction some hundred
miles west of Winnipeg. Persa took the most
direct, and, getting off the train before arriving
at the junction, she began to walk, making a wide
circuit. It was fortunate for her that she did
so, for her pursurers were there, meeting each
train from the West.

It was a raw March day when she started out
on the carriage road across the plains. The country is sparsely settled. Night overtook her before she reached a town, but she plodded on,
unafraid. Before setting out next morning she
was warned of an approaching blizzard, but she
refused to halt. The cold wind and long, slant-
ing sweep of snow soon enveloped her, blotting
out sky and road. It was only by the direction of
the blast, which luckily was at her back, that she
was able to maintain her sense of direction. As
it was, she was almost exhausted when she happened on a farmer who was bringing in some
cattle that had strayed in the storm. She had

passed close to his house without knowing it. The following day the blizzard had abated and the sympathetic Canadian offered to drive her to Winnipeg.

In the meantime Marko and Milano had quarreled, the former accusing the latter of being in love with the girl and causing his plan to fail. The father had returned to Saskatoon, where he preferred charges against Petri for obtaining money for a marriage which never took place. He had learned that Petri was in Montreal, where he had come from Nova Scotia with his wife, and had induced the Saskatoon police to telegraph an inspector of detectives to cause his arrest. This was done not so much to recover the money as to be avenged on the girl through her father and to positively annul the marriage of his son in the eyes of all gypsies and prevent the latter from possessing her.

Milano, however, had not given up all hope. He went to Winnipeg determined to watch the station and incoming trains. Such was his despair at the quarrel with his father and with having lost his bride that he began to drink. It was thus that he missed Persa when she resumed her journey.

By the time the train reached Montreal she was so spent by her travels and the aftereffects of the blizzard that she decided to stop there until she had somewhat recovered. Making inquiries in the district where the gypsies usually stay, she learned where some had been living, in an old shop in the slums, and went to the place.

Some faded calico draperies were hung across the window. What was her surprise on recognizing them! They belonged to her parents! She rushed to the door. It was locked. Beside herself with joy and impatience, she shook the latch with all her strength. *"Daia! Dade!"* she called. Why was it locked? Where was everyone? She was frightened now by the stillness. It was impossible to see in because of the hangings. She ran to the back door. It was firmly fastened. Was it all a dream? She was ill and her nerves were overwrought. By this time she was, indeed, almost delirious. The sudden joy and disappointment had been too great.

An Italian family next door found her sobbing on the doorstep. They answered her questioning with evasion and suspicion, but they finally told her that the gypsy who lived there had been arrested about a week before, for some reason, and that the preceding night the patrol had taken his wife away for fortune telling.

It was too late to be admitted to the jail that night, but in the morning she found her parents, and although their troubles were by no means over, what did they care as long as they were reunited? Soon after, Petri was absolved of the charge of obtaining money illicitly from Marko, and her mother was released after paying a fine for telling fortunes.

Petri's intentions had been entirely honest, but not so those of a tribe of Serbian gypsies whom I recently met in a camp in northern Illinois. There were some thirty tents pitched on a river bank on the edge of a state forest preserve. In spite of the fact that a number of the families were truly Romani, friendly and loyal, the band as a whole had been corrupted by the leader, a tall, well-built fellow, who obviously had an admixture of *Gajo* blood in his veins. He was the one gypsy whom I ever heard boast of having had an illicit affair with a Romani woman, and I was not surprised when I read in the newspapers that he had been arrested on the charge of deserting his wife and absconding with twenty thousand dollars from the "royal treasury."

They were evidently prosperous, for most of the autos that were standing beside the tents were high powered, high priced, and in fair condition. Money had not brought them much happiness, however, according to a gyspy with a long gray mustache and with a purple-silk scarf picturesquely knotted about his throat. He was sitting apart from the rest, and invited me to squat on the grass beside him. "It's a bad camp," he remarked, glad to find some one to whom he could relieve his feelings. "They're money mad. Always fighting. *Čingaren.*"

Most of the men were standing in a circle about two small boys who were wrestling. For some time they struggled, rolling over and over each other, pulling and straining without either one gaining decided advantage. "Let them decide which is the better by fist fight, *marelpé,*" some one suggested. *"Djas?"* ("Will you go to it?") asked the shorter and stockier of the two in deadly earnest. Seconds were chosen, a watch was held, and the two boys fought for twenty minutes, with short intermissions, until the taller finally admitted he was beaten. He gave in with tears in his eyes, and had to be held to keep from flying at another who taunted him with his defeat. Retiring to a safe distance, he picked up a stone, which he hurled at his tormentor, crying hysterically. Translating an American slang phrase into gypsy, the victor remarked, disdainfully, *"Dilo. Konik here!"* ("He's crazy. Nobody home!")

By this time the pugnacious instincts of the bystanders were all aroused. One of the men offered to wrestle another for five dollars, and a stalwart youth declared he would take on any two his own size.

I returned to the man in the purple scarf, who continued to express his indignation and to account for the prosperity of the tribe. "They are worse than *Gaje,*" he declared. *"Biken le borye trin štar var.* They sell their daughters as

[50]

brides three or four times. After a few months
or a year they take them back and sell them over
again. A fine thing for a gypsy to do," he
snorted, "worse than *Gaje!*"

An old woman sitting apart under a canvas
shelter about the size of a dog kennel asked to
whom he was talking, and, being told, "A strange
Romani," she called to me to come and sit beside
her, and poured forth her own lament. She was
nearly blind, and thrust her chin projecting from
toothless gums, her sunken, wrinkled cheeks, and
faded eyes with red rims, close to my face in a
vain attempt to see me. No wonder gypsy
women were often thought to be witches. There
was something owlish, uncanny in those peering
eyes that saw not. "No one comes near me,"
she moaned. Her life must have been an eternal
polar twilight, a joyless nothingness. "I am
useless to them," she said, with a hideous chuckle.
"Who would give any money for me?"

The fighting was over and the men had joined
a group of women sitting in the shade, sewing.
They called to me and began to quiz me, chiefly
with the idea of finding out if I had any cash.
Believing that I had, one of them proposed, without further ceremony, that I marry his sister.
He took me aside and told me that he would
persuade his father to let me have her cheap, if
I would give him something for making the
match, and called my attention to the fact that

her front teeth were all gold and that in one of them there was a diamond inset which showed when she smiled.

Seeing I was not impressed by her "dazzling" smile, another gypsy offered me a bargain in widows. She was seventeen and not bad-looking, he said, and offered to show her to me. As I did not show any interest, he resorted to a final argument, "There's an automobile that goes with her."

The examples which I have given present a rather unsavory picture of desertion and divorce among the gypsies, but they are certainly exceptional. I cite them merely as curiosities in human conduct. *"Le bonheur n'a pas d'histoire."* Fairy tales always *end* with a happy marriage, for the reason that happiness is of interest chiefly to those who enjoy it.

The true gypsy attitude toward marriage and divorce is summed up in the words of a Romani friend, a woman of strength and sweetness of character, who once said to me. "Man and wife is like the two wings of a bird. They don't need always to be together, 'cept when the bird's on the nest. But one's no good without the other. Look at my son. He divorced his wife some years back. She had her faults, but do you think he's happy now? You see him drinkin' and laughin', but he can't never forget; and when the whisky dies on him, and he wakes up, and it's all dark

[52]

The characteristic tserXe which they still use in Europe have been given up for tents of many forms. The shade of a tree, however, remains the favorite living room

in the tent and he's alone, he does a lot of thinkin'. I've heard him cry like a baby, and call out her name in his sleep."

As for the ceremonies connected with the marriage itself, a great many conflicting accounts have been given. This is not surprising, for a truly gypsy wedding consists in mating, much like the birds; but in every country, and in every tribe, special customs have been borrowed from the inhabitants, or have sprung up spontaneously. It is therefore impossible to generalize very freely.

The rites of the Spanish gypsies have been faithfully described by Borrow, but are becoming rarer and rarer. That they might have prevailed at one time among other Romanies is suggested by the fact that among the Nomads married women wear a crimson *diklo,* or kerchief, and that during a betrothal ceremony one is sometimes fastened to a pole in the center of the camp. The color may well be symbolic of the passing to wifehood. The custom of dancing on quantities of candy was paralleled as a huge joke at a Nomad wedding in Nova Scotia, by the couple dancing on a ton of onions.

Among the Anglo-American gypsies the proceedings are simplicity itself. Sometimes a boy will throw his hat on a girl's bed, but this is more with a view of compromising her and forcing her to marry him in order not to be talked about, than in fulfillment of a rite. A betrothal form occasionally used is, *"Mandv fer tuti"* and *"Tuti fer mandv."* Not infrequently they live together without being married by a minister or a justice of the peace, but in that case there is no ceremony.

These observations are substantiated by the remarks of a gypsy writer, the famous evangelist, Rodney Smith, as true a Romani as ever spoke Romanes: "Very often the sweethearting extends over a long period; they have grown up as sweethearts from boy and girl. . . . When the young people are able to set up for themselves they make a covenant with each other. Beyond this there is no marriage ceremony. . . . The ceremony is the same as that which was observed by Rebekah and Isaac. Isaac brought Rebekah into his tent, and she became his wife, and he lived with her. The gypsies are the most faithful and devoted husbands. I ought to add that the making of the marriage covenant is usually followed by a spree."

Among the Nomads there is a further similarity to Old Testament customs, in the payment of money for a bride. It is much as described in the biblical idyl of the Book of Ruth. "Moreover, Ruth the Moabitess, the wife of Mahlom, have I purchased to be my wife," Boaz declares before witnesses. "So Boaz took Ruth, and she became his wife."

Instead of resenting this, the average *bori* is proud of being valued at two or three thousand dollars. "How much did you pay for your wife?" one of them once asked me; and on being told that I had not paid anything, she looked at me with an expression of pity, as much as to say, "She must be a pretty poor wife, if you got her for nothing!"

The justification offered for this custom is the fact that a good fortune teller will make often hundreds of dollars for the husband or father in a single year, and the latter feels entitled to compensation for the loss of a breadwinner.

As the gypsies make more money in America than in Europe, the amount of compensation has increased exceedingly. Not long ago an old Nomad who was anxious to see his son married remarked to me in a mournful tone, "Daughters-in-law are getting awfully dear." Because of this a custom has sprung up, which does not prevail in Europe, I was told by a gypsy in Cincinnati, that before the married couple could save any money for themselves they were under obligation to pay back the purchase price to the groom's father.

The same Romani told me of a Syrian gypsy whom he knew, who had saved up two thousand dollars to get married. Remembering that he could marry for relatively little in the country from which he had come, and that the exchange was in his favor, he returned to Syria, bought a wife for a few dollars, spent the rest in having a good time, and returned to America with his bride.

As bride purchase also prevails to some extent among other gypsies than the Nomads—the Russian gypsy singers, for example—it is probable that it was once a general custom among Romanies. It is probable that it will die out in the country where it has been developed to the greatest extent—America. Gypsy girls are observing. Having seen the freedom of American women, many of them are beginning to revolt against a custom which smacks of slavery. Also, the coming in contact with other kinds of gypsies among whom it is not practiced to-day, is beginning to influence their ideas.

Art Smith, an English *Romaniĉel,* told me that a Russian gypsy had become enamored of his sister. His father was not disinclined toward the match until the Russian offered him two thousand dollars for the daughter. Insulted at the proposal that he sell her, he seized a pitchfork and drove him from the tent. All the Anglo-American Romanies, however, do not regard the custom in the same light. Only recently Frank Evans, a nineteen-year-old English *Romaniĉel,* paid two thousand five hundred dollars to John Mitchell, of the famous Nomad tribe, for his daughter, Mary, and five hundred dollars more for the wedding.

Like the Hindus, the gypsies spend huge sums on the feasting which follows both the betrothal and the marriage. When asked what the actual wedding ceremonies were, a Nomad woman replied to me, "Eating, drinking, fiddling, and dancing." Frequently a family will spend its last penny on these festivities. A collection, or *"dau,"* is taken up for the couple.

Perhaps it is these post-nuptial celebrations which have given rise to the current belief, expressed by Hugo in *Notre Dame de Paris,* that breaking a china crock is part of the rite. Wasting and smashing whatever lies at hand are part of the enjoyment in the lavish feasting which follows the simple unions.

What part love plays in these matches, which so resemble bargains, is hard for the *Gajo* to see; but the inclinations of the young people are usually consulted beforehand, and when they are not, love finds a way among the gypsies as among the *Gaje.* The extreme youth of the lovers would seem to indicate that their affection is mere puppy love, but we must not forget that the Romani matures with greater rapidity than other races, and that young love is often just as real as mature love, and always more intense and idealistic. No one doubts the love of Romeo and Juliet.

No amount of exposition is worth a concrete example. Let me therefore relate a story of gypsy love which happened a few years ago, in which I played a minor rôle.

CHAPTER III

THE ILIAD OF ELENA MIKE

TO-DAY the men of civilized races fight for petroleum, coal, and markets for their manufactured goods; their grandfathers fought for political principles; their great-great-grandfathers for the mere love of fighting. The gypsies care nothing for commerce, nothing for abstract principles, and why should they enjoy fighting for its own sake when their lives are a constant struggle with nature and the *Gaje*. But there is one thing for which the peace-loving gypsies will wage war. Like the ancient Greeks at Troy, they have fought again and again for a beautiful woman.

It was the second evening of the three-day celebration of the betrothal of my friend Nikola to the lovely sixteen-year-old Elena. They were both members of Nomadic bands that had traveled through most of Europe and the two Americas, and had made Chicago the center of their latest wanderings.

Some dozen tents were pitched in parallel lines on a low wooded knoll. In the middle a great fire

was blazing, giving warmth, light, and beauty.
It shone on the olive rose of the Romani faces,
on the tawny soil of the naked sand, and the
brownish purple of the leaves that fluttered as
they clung to the gnarly branches in the cold
November wind. It was a weird spot on the edge
of the dunes, at the lower end of Lake Michigan,
some miles across the state line from Illinois.
The nearest habitation was a solitary roadhouse,
seldom frequented and suspected of being a
refuge for hold-up men. The knoll, with its
sparse, hardy grass and scrub oaks, was one of
the countless waves of sand.

For ages and ages the region had been deserted. Even the Indians had used it only as a
hiding place from their enemies. And now the
desolate scene had burst into seething animation.

In front of the large tent belonging to Elena's
father, the chief of the tribe, a crimson *diklo,*
fastened to a pole, was waving and dancing in
the breeze, as though with joy. Orange is an
adequate symbol, perhaps, of *Gajo* love. But
nothing short of crimson pictures the intensity
of gypsy passion.

On the opposite side of the fire an orchestra
of Hungarian gypsies was playing with dash and
abandon. At the last minute some one had discovered them in a saloon in South Chicago, playing to the "Hunkies" from the steel mills, and
had engaged them in place of a Polish band that

The hair is usually braided and oiled, sometimes in four braids, with coins and pieces of silk woven into the strands

had previously been hired. The first violin, the leader, was from the Banat, and played a great number of Slavic, Magyar, and Rumanian songs and dances, as well as many that were purely Romani. The cembalist, the second violin, and the bass viol played the accompaniments as though by instinct, following the leader through a maze of unfamiliar melodies. If there was a song he did not know, a chorus of gypsies would sing it for him. With his violin tucked under one arm, he would listen intently to one or two stanzas, then draw his bow across the strings in a strong wide sweep that was a signal to his men, and begin the music with as much sureness as though he had known it all his life.

A Hungarian song was played:

> *"Devla! Devla! So me kerdiom?"*
> ("God! O God! What have I done?")

It was a tragic song; for the moment the gay circle was hushed. The steel strings of the cembalo rang like a soft thunder, as the player with his padded sticks beat a wild tattoo; or, as he swung them here and there over the entire instrument, they seemed to dance in mockery of the long lament of the violin. There was something cosmic in the music. It was intended for the out-of-doors. It was like the wind in the branches above us, the wind that was piling the sand in giant waves on the edge of the inland sea,

trumpeting the storms of winter, and flying end-
lessly through the darkness of the prairie night.
The seated figures swayed their bodies with the
music; uplifted arms slowly waved from side to
side, as though groping hopelessly for something
intangible.

The tempo changed. Now it was a song half
sad, half gay:

"Romané čukeya uglatinén."

The rhythm shifted from an allegretto to a
mad scherzo, and several of the gypsies jumped
to their feet and began a wild czardas, stamping,
leaping, and whirling in a frenzy of gayety.

The orchestra began a different dance melody,
something like the Serbian kolo. Putting their
arms about one another's shoulders, they all
formed a circle about the fire, revolving for a
few steps in one direction, then in the reverse.
They kicked and sprang, as though unable to
restrain their joy; they bent forward as though
bowed over by winds of passion, then backward,
with breast and face skyward as though in ex-
ultant abandon.

The scene was barbaric. The black hair of the
Romanies melted into the blackness of the night.
The firelight gleamed in flashing eyes. It shone
on the red coral, the large yellow beads, and the
necklaces of golden coins of the women. Their red
and orange dresses turned and twisted like the

[62]

tongues of flame. Two little tots had taken their mothers' crimson *diklos* and were dancing voluptuously, prolonging the undulations of their supple bodies with the snake-like movements of the kerchiefs.

There was nothing of solemn mystery in the betrothal celebration of these Romanies. The thoughts of the young leaped forward to the time when they, too, should mate. The older couples renewed their passion, and nature itself, fanning the flames, seemed animated with the vital surge.

From time to time I glanced at the betrothed couple. Sometimes they appeared rapturously happy, and then again they seemed unable to believe their senses, as though their happiness were too great to last.

I had missed the ceremonies of the preceding day: the payment of fifteen hundred dollars and the swearing of the oath to mate and be true to each other. There had been some trouble in regard to the negotiations, I was told, because of some difference in regard to the total amount which the groom's father was to pay; but the difficulties had been settled and the feasting had continued.

At one end of the camp was a trench of live coals, over which a whole pig, a sheep, and several turkeys were roasting on spits, turned by the children. It was a lark for the little ones. Under

[63]

the direction of the men, they brought fresh coals from the bonfire and clapped their hands and shouted when the fat from the roasts dripped on the fire and blazed up fiercely. What a tantalizing odor of browned meat drifted past the tents!

But there was no need for being tantalized for long. There was no special hour for banqueting; the entire three days were one prolonged feast. Each person ate whenever he was hungry, whenever some morsel he had been watching was done, or whenever he was invited into one of the tents, where chickens were stewing in inviting soups, and bread and cakes were piled on trays. The gypsies ate with a joy in the profusion, which can only be felt by those who more than once have suffered the pangs of hunger. It was a three-day banquet.

If the feasting was Homeric, the drinking was truly Gargantuan. In one tent a huge keg of beer foamed into cups, glasses, buckets, and tea-kettles. In every tent was a case of beer, a gallon or two of red wine, or a bottle of metaxa, their favorite brandy. A pavilion large enough to contain some fifty people had been set up for the Chief MiXail, Elena's father; and there with his own hand he poured an excellent Bordeaux into tiny silver cups and a huge loving cup, hand wrought and very old, which was passed from guest to guest.

MiXail le Worsosko, better known by his *Gajikano* name, Mike Mitchell, was tall, and although he was beginning to develop a paunch, he was still extremely powerful. He was proud, stubborn, and combative. He was tyrannical with his family and his tribe, self-centered and blustery, but good natured as long as he had his own way. His enemies accused him of being overfond of money, but no one accused him of being stingy. His father had been a bear leader, and he had grown up with bears, very much like one of them; in fact, his nickname, was *O Mečko,* The Bear. His wife, Marya, was always easygoing, lazy, and negative. She was fond of her children and of her husband. She considered the latter a very superior being and took a certain pleasure in humbling herself before him. She feared him as a savage fears his gods.

I had known them for two years and had always been a welcome guest. They were one of the first families of Nomads that I had met. Following a group of them to a house off Blue Island Avenue, Chicago, I finally gathered up courage to knock on the door. It was opened by MiXail in shirt sleeves, wearing a watch chain as big as a rope. He towered above me and demanded in a loud, rough voice what I wanted. I wanted to run away, but I told him that I was looking for my people. *"Kalo Rom san tu?"* he asked. Unsuccessfully, I tried to explain the

variety of gypsy I was, but the chief, nevertheless, invited me to enter, with gruff friendliness.

Since then I had seen them two or three times
and had written a love letter for Elena to Nikola,
the man to whom she had just been betrothed.
She was sixteen and extremely beautiful, slender,
delicately featured, and with a soft glow in her
cheeks which was very striking in one so dark.
She was a strange combination of shyness and
impulse, eager to live, but restrained by her very
sensitiveness. She seemed surrounded by an
aura of invisible flame.

"Janes tu lil?" she asked me one day when I
came to her father's tent. I admitted that I
could write and granted her request to transcribe
a letter to Nikola, her sweetheart. As it is rare
indeed to find a gypsy who is literate, most
letters are written for them by *Gaje,* in English.
It is quite confusing to take the dictation, as the
entire camp joins in, suggesting phrases and
canceling others. As there is no secrecy in gypsy
love-making, Elena could not tell me what she
wanted to say without half a dozen simultaneous
suggestions from the group of youngsters who
had gathered about me. Half a dozen times I
was interrupted by requests to read what I had
already taken down, as each one was proud of
hearing his sentiments expressed in writing and
suspicious that I might be adding something on
my own account. Finally I closed with the

[66]

words of Elena herself, "I love you with all my heart."

As yet I had not made the acquaintance of Nikola, or "Kolya," as he was familiarly called. The family was in California at the time; but on his return to Chicago I had met him at the Mitchells', and in the few times we saw each other, before the betrothal ceremony, we had become such good friends that he had suggested that I drop my *Gajo*-sounding name and take his own.

He was an affectionate fellow, about twenty-two years old, energetic and daring, a good hater and a good lover. I have never seen him show fear. Sitting on the grass in front of the tent one day, we heard a blood-curdling sound, half whinny, half squeal. Two stallions were fighting. Without hesitation, he jumped up and separated the infuriated animals that were wheeling about each other, raining terrific blows with their steel-shod heels.

Nikola's father was a gypsy of the old school—lazy and good natured, spending his money as fast as his wife made it. It had not been easy for him to accumulate the sum which MiXail demanded. I was therefore pleased to see the lovers finally betrothed, especially as I was fond of them both and imagined I had had a finger in the courtship.

At the time, I was studying for a master's

[67]

degree at the University of Wisconsin. One Friday afternoon, late in November, I had barely had time to catch a train for Chicago, at the close of a seminar. On arriving at the northwestern station, I went at once to the "Workingmen's Exchange," at Halstead and Monroe, to see if I could get in touch with any gypsies. A Romani, known to the *Gaje* as Mexican Pete, was drinking by himself at the bar. In reply to my inquiries, he told me of the betrothal celebration, but advised me not to attend it. His tone, as he said this, was intended to be mysterious and was a trifle sneering. Mexican Pete was a disagreeable fellow and not very popular with his fellow Romanies. He had quarreled with Nikola, and for this reason I attributed his remarks to his dislike, and thought no more of the matter.

How I congratulated myself on coming in time to see most of the festivities!

The dancing continued, although it was past midnight and the musicians had been playing since morning, with few intervals of rest. To keep them going in the proper mood, the liquor which was poured so freely to the other gypsies was served to them in carefully calculated doses —Greek brandy and black coffee every so often. But as the Nomads themselves grew more intoxicated and less able to dance through sheer exhaustion, they allowed the musicians to have what they wanted. A "box" of beer was placed on the ground beside the cembalo. The second violin, who was blind from birth and simple-minded, knowing but few pleasures in life besides his music, knelt beside the case and, putting his arms around the necks of the bottles, kissed one tenderly on the mouth. In his haste to open a bottle, the bass viol tore off the metal cap with his teeth.

The music grew wilder and the shouts of the Romanies more furious. As the few inhibitions were removed, half-suppressed animosities flared up. Dzurka, a gypsy who had asked for Elena's hand the year before and had been refused, began to make trouble. He had been refused partly because Elena had not cared for him—he was twice her age—and partly because the sum he had offered did not suit her father. In the meantime, however, he had grown rich, or rather his father had grown rich, which was the same thing, his mother through *čoripe,* having recently fleeced a *Gajo* of two or three thousand dollars. The refusal had hurt his pride. Perhaps, too, he had loved the girl, who was certainly attractive enough to arouse a tender passion in as rough and vindictive a breast as Dzurka's.

One of the latter's closest friends was a certain Groffo, a practical joker with a cruel streak like Dzurka, and quite as crafty. He was less fond of fighting than Dzurka, but he was always egg-

ing others on. That night one or two battles
had been narrowly averted, partly owing to the
fact that gypsy tempers cool as quickly as they
kindle, partly to the women and older men, who
were less intoxicated and threw themselves between the quarrelsome.

The cold night wind whipping the bent
branches had increased from half a gale to a
gale. Reading the signs in the sky, even the most
preoccupied and heedless of the gypsies had long
since tightened the tent ropes and given the pegs
an extra blow. Even so, stray pieces of canvas
flapped with a swift vibrato, and branches overhead hummed in the wind. It was all the musicians could do to overtop the sounds of nature.
There were moments when only the shrill cry
of the first violin could be heard. More and
more the strings of the instruments and the players themselves seemed a part of the growing
storm.

The sound of shouts, cries of joy and of pro-
test from somewhere behind the tents, suddenly
dominated all others. I followed the swarm of
gypsies that scrambled to watch what was going
on, and saw a crowd emerge into the open space.
In the midst of the ant-like moving mass, Groffo
was leading an old nag that belonged to Nikola.

In the early Vedic period of Hindu history,
more than a thousand years before Christ, before
any known date, the Indo-Aryan tribes sacrificed

The beauty of gypsy women matures
very rapidly, but their charm
is always young

"Ma mara les!" ("Don't you hit him!") the latter shouted.

"Tut marav!" ("I'll hit you, if you don't get out!") was Nikola's reply.

Before he could act, several of the older men had seized his arms and dragged him through the crowd, which immediately closed again in a solid circle. They argued with him to convince him that Groffo and Dzurka had meant no harm, and that the killing of the horse would bring him luck, and that the nag was not worth anything, anyway.

Dzurka had drawn a long knife, that gleamed in the moonlight as he raised it above his head. At a backward sweep of his arm, and the flourish of the blade the ring suddenly widened. The gypsy stood back a pace, then threw himself on the animal, stabbing it. A stream of blood shot from below the shoulder. There was a brief silence. The horse fell heavily. Shouts of fear, horror, and triumph merged in a single yell that made the flesh creep.

Dzurka, covered with blood, knife in hand, stood in the center of the widened circle.

Tearing himself free from the restraining arms, Nikola whipped out his own knife and plunged forward. The crowd opened with instinctive terror, but it closed immediately about the two men, who were forced to grapple. A dozen hands pulled them apart. Elena had followed close beside Nikola. Throwing her arms about him, she felt some blood on his coat.

A piercing shriek. Slowly she slipped to the ground, unconscious.

It was the blood of the horse that had smeared him in the tussle with Dzurka. He was unhurt and, lifting her in his arms, he carried her to her father's tent.

The great fire, which had been allowed to die down, and the moon, which plunged at frequent intervals beneath the purple edges of the flying clouds, were the only sources of light on the wild scene. The Hungarian musicians, who had remained somewhat in the background, were not sure of what had happened. They had caught a glimpse of the knifeplay, the slain horse, and the limp form of a woman carried across the open space. It was enough. They were house-dwellers, separated for generations from their untamed brothers, whose barbarity their child-like imaginations magnified with terror.

Without a thought of his pay, the leader started to run, with his violin case under one arm, and the instrument under the other. The bass viol followed as well as he could, his huge viol flung on his back, thumping him at every step. The cembalo player, deathly afraid, but unwilling to abandon his instrument, remained with the blind musician, who sensed the trouble from the

[73]

groped their way to the open, but luckily it put an end to the fighting.

MiXail commanded everyone to retire, and he and his family sought shelter in the quarters of his brother. What with the fierce gale raging outside and the excitement of the stirring incidents of the night, there were not many who slept.

Nikola had previously asked me to share his tent, but the recent events had naturally driven all thought of me from his mind, and I hesitated about intruding. Fortunately, his father, Giorgi, remembered, and drew me inside, giving me a thick feather bed for mattress, and another for a covering.

Morning must have dawned soon after, though it seemed like a long time. Nikola's mother, Mitra, who was somewhat ill tempered for a gypsy, had gotten up and was poking at the fire and scolding.

The children had begun to run in and out, clad in little or nothing. I rose and glanced toward Nikola. He was gazing upward with wide-open, unseeing eyes, his forehead contracted in a frown. As he did not seem to hear my "Good morning," I stepped outside.

The wind was less powerful, but it still rushed and roared from off the Great Lakes, and the morning was cold and gloomy. The dead horse lay in a pool of frozen blood. The collapsed tent

was billowing and flapping. The jagged end of
the broken pole had torn a gash that was constantly widening. The chief's brother, Ilía, aided
by Dzurka and Groffo, were fastening it, and
discussing something with great earnestness.
When I approached and offered to help, they refused somewhat gruffly and became silent. The
three of them entered Ilía's tent, where MiXail
and Elena had taken refuge; and a quarter of an
hour later, when they came out, Dzurka was
smiling, but his smile was not pleasant to see.

Soon after, he and his companions had left.

No one was in a good humor, but Nikola's de-
pression and anxiety were pitiful. His temperament was extraordinarily sensitive and mobile;
and except when roused, or in the face of physical
danger, he was rather diffident. The usual
spring was lacking in his step as he crossed the
open space toward the tent of his betrothed.
Ilía met him and barred the entrance with a flood
of excuses. Then he took him aside and argued
with him for some time.

Nikola returned more downcast than before,
and after a consultation with his father it was
decided that they should leave.

The tent, a trunk, and heaps of bedding were
piled into the covered wagon, the remaining horse
was tied to the rack behind, and we were off.
With Nikola and the children I lay on the feather
beds, which reached nearly to the top of the

South Chicago, with nothing to vary the cramped view but blackened factory walls, red gas tanks, and an occasional church steeple. Next day I was back in the routine of classes and study.

I was trying to plan a thesis, "A Comparison of the Love Elements in the Iliad and 'Tristan and Iseult'"; but the thoughts of Nikola and Elena occupied my mind, excluding those of the famous lovers of antiquity. As soon as the Christmas vacation arrived, I returned to Chicago.

In a Halsted Street car was a crowd of Nomads, jabbering in Romanes. Halsted Street is used to strange sights and queer tongues, but all the *Gajos* were staring; and some one with a strong foreign accent remarked, "Aw, why don't dey talk Amurcan?" It was not a favorable place to approach them, so I waited until they got off. They sensed that I had followed them and were somewhat suspicious, but one of the men finally told me that there was a camp at the end of the Archer Avenue line.

Arriving there, I found some scattered tents, rickety wagons, and shaggy ponies with their winter coats ruffled by the biting wind. I had hoped to find Nikola, and, to my delight, he was there. His face beamed with gladness for a moment. When I asked about Elena, his features flashed with pain and bitterness.

"Do not mention her name, brother!"

*Food is served at any and all hours.
The triangular iron makes a good
portable stove*

washing some clothes. Silver bands and bracelets standing out against her bare dark arms vaguely shone through the vapor. In a corner the mother sat on her calves with her knees to her chin, smoking a long pipe which nearly touched the ground. Her dress was bright red with wide yellow sleeves, that hung in plaits.

Except when she slowly puffed her pipe, she was as silent and immutable as a graven idol. It was a striking picture, as I see it now, dim and mellow, yet rich and brilliant, like a painting by an old master, a Rembrandt or a Tintoretto, or like gypsy life itself, always gay or somber— or both. At the time, I was thinking only of how I could help Nikola and cheer him up.

At a roadhouse opposite the camp I got two bottles of port wine and sang an English-gypsy song, *"Lel a čuma, del a čuma,"* to the amusement of the circle. A tiny youth, after some encouragement, gave another *Romani ghili,* and after the wine had passed a few times, the ice that had frozen Kolya's spirits began to thaw, and he gave expression to his sadness. He had traveled through Spain and South America years before, and some ancient, half-forgotten coplas came to his lips on waves of plaintive melody, partly Moorish, partly gypsy. He sang of how the love that had been like wine, sweet and intoxicating, was now like vinegar; of how the glad songs he had once composed for his sweetheart and had sung with joyous rapture, were now the saddest that he knew; of how he longed for sleep to ease his sorrow, but in vain, for sleep brought dreams of her. A final copla, in Spanish, with a slight admixture of gypsy, relieved his feelings somewhat; but his grief was too recent, too powerful, to be helped for long by mere expression.

> " 'Mal haya er dinero,
>   Que er dinero es causa
> Que los sacais de quien yo camelo
>   No estén en mi casa!' "

> (" 'A curse upon thee, money,
>   For all because of thee
> The eyes of her I dearly love
>   No longer dwell with me!' ")

He became silent again, his eyes fixed unseeingly on the dim canvas wall.

"I have a plan," I suggested. Nikola paid no attention, so I decided to say no more until I was sure of at least being able to attempt it.

By various inquiries I managed to find Elena telling fortunes with her mother in a small curtained booth in a shooting gallery on Halsted Street near Monroe. I went in and, pretending not to have heard the news, I asked, "How is Nikola?"

"Či janav" ("I don't know"), she answered, and her eyes suddenly moistened.

"Where can I find him?"

She started to reply, but her voice was too full and she merely shook her head. Here was good news. Elena still loved him. `If only I could get rid of her mother for a moment. Unmarried girls are carefully watched, and, although Marya doubtless sympathized with her daughter, she was responsible to MiXail for her safe-keeping, and she was too much in awe of him to dare rebel.

I went to the keeper of the gallery, took a quarter's worth of shots and leisurely began firing, looking about the place and questioning the man about the gypsies. I found that there was a door leading to an alley, and learned that each noon the mother was accustomed to go across the street to a lunch room for sandwiches. The next thing was to get hold of Nikola at once. Vaguely I recalled the name of the roadhouse-keeper in gold letters on black. It began with Z and, to my dismay, I found that in the Chicago telephone directory Z was as plentiful as water in Lake Michigan. By comparing each Z with the approximate number on Archer Avenue I finally found it. The barkeeper gruffly refused to call Kolya to the telephone until told that it was a matter of life and death, as indeed it was. "Meet me at Madison and Canal at noon," I told him. He was not easily persuaded, but my tones, perhaps, rather than my words, made him realize how important it was, and he promised to be

there. Next, I went to the Workingmen's Exchange, a saloon on the corner near the shooting
gallery. It would have been unwise for me to
take the message myself to Elena, telling her
to meet Nikola, since the mother was sure to
keep her eye on the booth and connect my entrance not only with the daughter's disappearance, but also with Nikola. There was an old
man, whom many people will remember, who
used to stand on the corner in front of the saloon,
selling roses and carnations. His hair and mustache, which were white, stood out against his
features, as pink as one of his own flowers. He
was to be the message bearer.

I knew it would not be easy to persuade him.
Most people have an unreasoning fear of gypsies; nothing could persuade them to risk interfering in their affairs. The old man was an
Oriental, and I felt sure that there was a poetic
corner somewhere in his heart. Like Hafiz and
Omar, he had two passions, wine and roses. I
invited him to have several drinks at the bar,
and bought out his entire stock of flowers, taking
only a few. Then I asked him to watch until the
older gypsy woman crossed the street and then
to deliver the following words: "Meet Nikola at
once at Canal and Madison." Supposing I myself was carrying on an intrigue with the girl,
he smiled sympathetically, and was finally persuaded. If the mother questioned him, he was to

complain that the girl had taken his money for telling his fortune and had suddenly decamped.

At twelve o'clock I was at the appointed place. Nikola had already been waiting some time. He had guessed that the rendezvous had something to do with his betrothed, and had come at once, in spite of the fact that he had indicated that he hated her and never wanted to hear her name again. When I told him of the unmistakable signs of love Elena had manifested, I thought he, too, would weep—for joy.

When I unfolded my plan—a marriage by the justice of the peace—Kolya was stunned. He declared that it was a serious breach of the law of his tribe, a defiance of the whole social organization of the Nomads. He and his bride would be outcasts. I pointed out, in reply, that according to the gypsy law of most tribes the betrothal ceremony was practically equivalent to a marriage, and that in reality they were already married, and that once they were married by American law, no power could keep them apart. This reassured him. Still, I am sure he would have gone through with it without my persuasion.

A half hour went by, and no bride. My friend was in agonies of doubt. Poor fellow! What if I had raised his hopes in vain? Or what if the girl had been overtaken? Perhaps the message had miscarried. I had given up hope, but not Nikola. I think he would have waited there for hours.

At last he caught sight of her bright dress a block away through the crowd. I could hardly keep him from running full speed to join her. Such joy as they met! They were drunk with happiness, oblivious of everything. But there was no time to spare. We must act at once, heartless though it seemed to interrupt their ecstasy and bring them to their senses.

Elena was told of the scheme. It was more of a shock to her than it had been to Kolya. Her deep love for her father and mother, her awe of the latter and the veneration for gypsy custom that was part of her very blood, struggled with her love. It was pitiful to see her inner anguish. I had counted on the presence of the betrothed, however, and the look of tender appeal in his eyes won.

Immediately, we went to the City Hall and took out a marriage license. The thought suddenly struck me that Elena was under age. However, it was too late to turn back. Under the very nose of the clerk I said to her, *"De duma kai san tu dešoXtengri."* And with the greatest assurance she informed him that she was eighteen.

It was some time before they could be married. The couple attracted considerable attention in the corridors outside the court room.

"I wonder what they are being tried for?" I overheard a passer-by remark.

"Tried!" his companion ejaculated, glancing at the radiant smile of the two gypsies. "It looks to me more like they'd inherited a million dollars."

When their turn came the judge's set expression melted. It was evidently a welcome variation from the regular grist of affairs. "We want to marry, American fashion," Elena announced to the magistrate.

"Do you love this man?" he asked the girl. Elena's only answer was to throw her arms joyously around Kolya's neck. The ceremony was performed immediately.

There was a certain amount of misgiving as to how even Kolya's relatives would consider a *Gajikanes* wedding. Nevertheless, they decided to start for the camp at once. Lights in the office buildings of the cañons of the Loop began to shine high up on the blackened walls. The sun, a ball of red fire, pierced the gray mist and smoke at the end of a long level street. Over the slowly moving tide of pedestrians and autos on State Street, I saw them board an Archer Avenue car. Elena turned and waved good-by with the bunch of roses I had bought from the flower seller. It was the last I saw of them for some time.

Opening a newspaper one morning, I was attracted by an item copied from a Chicago paper. "Marriage of gypsy princess set aside by court." It related how "Princess Helen Mike, a striking beauty, who eloped with Nikolas George a month ago, has been reclaimed by her father, whose petition that the marriage was illegal, owing to the age of the sixteen-year-old bride, was sustained by the court, after a lively legal battle. The bride was carried from the court room in a dead faint."

A fine ending for their romance! In spite of the slight changes in the names, there was no doubt but that it referred to my friends.

Easter Sunday I was in Chicago, half hoping, half fearing to meet them once more. Starting for the West Side on foot, I stopped for a moment on the Twelfth Street viaduct to watch the scene—the wall-like sky line, the snowy roofs of the freight sheds, the solid black of a huge grain elevator, row on row of polished steel rails leading thither, the spidery framework of the bridge, the muddy river with cakes of green ice sluggishly floating lakeward, and white gulls restlessly wheeling with weird cries.

Shortly afterward, on Twelfth Street, I overtook a little gypsy girl carrying a load of kindling wood on her head. It was a younger sister of Nikola. She accompanied me to a house on Jefferson Street, to which they had been driven by prolonged zero weather. Kolya was not there, though the house was crowded with friends celebrating Easter, which is one of the most important festivals among the gypsies. I learned that Elena had run away and that she and Nikola were in hiding.

Two hours later, walking through the Maxwell Street district, I saw by the characteristic hangings in the window of a house that it was inhabited by Romanies. I entered without knocking, and with something of a shock I found myself in the presence of MiXail, Dzurka, and the rest of the band. Their greeting showed that Elena had kept secret my part in the affair; but nevertheless, they were not very cordial. It was a dingy sort of a palace for a "king"— broken floor, wall paper hanging in strips, and in one of the windows, opaque with grime, a hole had been mended by stuffing it with rags. I was given the one seat, an empty beer case. For some reason they were not celebrating the holiday. There was an atmosphere of preparation and bustle. The chief was shaving in front of a fragment of mirror nailed to the wall.

At a hint that they had business elsewhere, I got up and left, glad of an excuse, and started back to the house of Nikola's father. From the Twelfth Street car I noticed gypsy boys running along the sidewalk, gleefully whacking the iron telegraph poles with clubs.

The all-day feast was still going on when I
returned. I was asked once more to join them,
Giorgi himself filling a glass of wine for me from
a stone jug. Five minutes later a boy standing
at the window shouted excitedly, *"Aven!"*
("They're coming!")

"Kon?"

"MiXail!"

The gypsies leaped to their feet. The chief
appeared at the door, armed with his silver-
headed *busdegan,* his staff of office, ready for an
attack; but MiXail gravely announced that he
had come for a parley (*diwano*), not for a fight.

No sooner did Dzurka see me than he scowled
and stepped forward threateningly. He evidently thought that I had gone to spy on them,
and had hurried back to report. "What are you
doing here?" he growled. My reply half satisfied
him, and he squatted on the floor with the others,
in the closely packed circle. Not being invited
to join them, I remained with the woman and
children in a small room opening on a larger one.

The council began. It was dominated by the
chief, a head taller than the rest. One after another was granted permission to speak. It was
difficult to hear everything from where I stood,
but I caught the words, *"Gajikano kris* and *Romano kris"* ("Gentile court and gypsy court"),
repeated again and again, together with the
names of Elena, Nikola, and Dzurka. Both sides

[91]

were reproaching the other for not settling the affair among themselves instead of appealing to outsiders.

For a while all was fairly peaceful and orderly, but soon voices rose, fists pounded the floor, and some one jumped to his feet. There was a moment of confusion. I felt myself almost lifted from my feet, half carried to the back door by the powerful arms of Mitra, Nikola's mother, and firmly pushed outside. As the door slammed, I found myself sprawling on a heap of ashes, a dead rat, and various unmentionable rubbish in the alley. I picked myself up and retreated, with more haste than dignity. For a moment I debated as to whether or not it was my duty to return and take my part in the trouble I had helped to start, but I concluded that Mitra knew what she was doing.

At 2 A.M., when I unfolded a newspaper in the train to kill time during the long, slow ride back to Madison, I read the following article:

ELOPEMENT OF PRINCESS CAUSES BATTLE OF RIVAL CLANS

. . . With a score of loyal subjects King Mike Mitchell laid siege to the rival fortress. When police reserves arrived every man, woman, child, and dog was giving battle. The king's forces were getting the worst of it. A lull in the hostilities was forced by the bluecoats and a number of the combatants were interned in the police station to preserve neutrality. Both sides declared complete satisfaction to have been obtained and a feud of long standing to be over. The princess, who appeared with her *fiancé* during the fighting, was slightly wounded, but refused to go to the hospital. She was given the paternal blessing.

At last, after various futile interventions of *Gajo* law, the lovers had finally won in the gypsy court of ultimate appeal—a battle royal.

In May, I found them in camp once more, on the western outskirts of the city. Soon after Easter, Nikola's father had paid the sum demanded by MiXail; and a big wedding, "gypsy fashion" this time, had been celebrated.

"It is lucky you came to-day," Nikola remarked. "A day later you wouldn't have found us."

We sat on the prairie grass, studded with wild flowers, and they told me of all that had happened since I saw them last.

In the morning I watched their caravan pull out along a road bordered with flowering thorn apple.

"Del O Del baXt!" ("God give you luck!") I called after them.

"God give you a wife like Elena—and children!" Nikola shouted, as they waved good-by.

CHAPTER IV

How fortunes are told; and children are not kidnapped.

FOR all that Karlo Bimbo had given me minute instructions and that I had had much experience in finding gypsy camps, it was only after considerable search that I finally discovered the carefully concealed tents of Woršo and his band in a field near South Chicago, one afternoon in August, a few years ago. Billboards and clumps of dense trees hid them from houses and a near-by street car line. On the opposite side lay the level prairie, its green expanse dotted with tiny flowers. On the horizon rose the blank wall of a huge storehouse, the giant torch of a blast furnace, and the delicate steel lacework of some docks soaring above an invisible canal. In another direction lay Lake Michigan, its white waves flashing in long rows across the wide blue surface.

Woršo and his son, Stivo, were relatives of my friend Kolya, and I knew them slightly. As I

[94]

*The delicate steel lacework of some docks,
South Chicago*

approached, I saw some children playing with
the horses, riding bareback. In one of the tents
a girl was oiling and combing her long black
tresses. In another the men were reclining on
soft cushions and passing the time with thoughts
as lazy as the smoke that curled from their
cigarettes, as magnificently idle as the flowers
and the clouds. *"Ušti p'uro Rom!"* ("Get up
for the old gypsy!") said Woršo to a boy,
motioning to me to take his seat on a cushion.
I was still in the twenties, but older than the boy;
and age constitutes a hierarchy among the
gypsies.

They had heard that I was a fortune teller
and were curious to see a Romani who preferred
to be one himself, instead of simply marrying and
letting his wife support him by the art. *Sar
keres? Po vast, po šero?"* ("How do you do it?
By palmistry, by phrenology?")

"No," I replied, *"po sune"* ("by dreams").
Nine-tenths of all fortune telling is an exhibition
of skill in extracting money rather than in rend-
ing secrets from the future. It is also an exhibition of character reading, which in the case of
certain Romanies I know is nothing short of
miraculous. By long practice they have cultivated their powers of observation and sub-
conscious reasoning to a degree that makes an
open book of the entire person to whom they are
giving a "reading." As they themselves are not

always conscious of how they do it, they attribute their remarkable powers to supernatural causes; and thus a few *dŭkkerers* believe that if they so desire they can tell "true" fortunes. Likewise, many gypsies believe in the truth of dreams, though they use them also to hoax.

When I spoke of *sune* they became interested, and asked if I could *drabarav čačes*. I answered that I could, being desirous of demonstrating I was a Romani, and of trying a new experiment. At the time I was steeped in Freudian psychology. I had attended lectures on abnormal psychology under Janet in Paris, and Jastrow at Wisconsin, and had studied everything that had been written by or about Freud and the symbolism and interpretation of dreams. The gypsies have evolved a system of symbols far in advance of the so-called gypsy dream books, which are pure nonsense; but their methods are crude and of little value. I might add that the technique of psycho-analysis is of little value in fortune telling, except in telling the fortunes of gypsies. Many sittings would be necessary to penetrate their inner life, were it not for the fact that Romanies are like children, the least suppressed, perhaps, of any living race. Their dreams are relatively simple and direct.

It may be also that luck was with me. Unsuspectingly, Stivo offered to tell me his dreams.

Stivo, eldest son of Woršo, was an energetic,

ambitious young Nomad, who resembled his father through his firm will. Woršo was elderly, with streaks of steel gray in his hair and mustache. He was the leader of a small clan which he ruled with an inexorable domination which must have chafed his resolute son. Stivo's mother had resembled her husband too closely, and had run away; whereupon Woršo had taken a young and pretty wife, not much older than Stivo, and wholly pliant to her husband's whims.

Owing to the respect he felt for his father, the natural filial affection, very strong in this race, and to the traditional giving in of the younger to the older, there had never been an open break between them. But a storm was brewing below the surface, a storm of which neither was aware. It was clearly indicated by the nature of the recurring dreams, which Stivo related with the utmost frankness, little realizing their purport.

It was chiefly a case of offended self-regard or pride, repressed ambition, a common phenomenon, but one which has never had the proper attention of the psychologists. It was further complicated by the attractiveness of Woršo's youthful wife.

I foretold a serious quarrel between father and son, and a distant separation. Any separation between such widely traveling Nomads was sure to be distant. The gypsies were skeptical of my prediction, and highly amused. It did not add to my credit as a teller of fortunes.

Some years later I met Nikola, and in talking over the news of various mutual acquaintances he asked if I had heard about Stivo and Worso. Shaking his head in disapproval at the mere thought of it, he related how they had had a fight and how Stivo had denounced his father to the federal authorities for secretly crossing the Mexican border without a passport. As it was during the war, it was a serious offense, and after detaining the old man in prison for a while, the authorities deported him to Serbia, the country from which he had come to the United States many years before and where it would be extremely difficult to make a living at that moment.

The crime of denouncing one's own father to the law was so unheard of among the gypsies that Stivo had been made practically an outcast. "Worse than a *Gajo!*" Kolya repeated, bitterly. "Worse than a *Gajo!*" is a term of utmost reproach, as though there was nothing worse than a non-gypsy. Great indeed must have been the quarrel to determine Stivo to resort to such desperate measures. I wonder if he remembers the prophecy?

Fortune telling is an art that the gypsies brought from India, the home of the occult and the mysterious. They practice many different forms of it, of which palmistry is the favorite. But whatever the Romani seeress may say about "heart lines" and "mounts of Saturn" to a person she is "reading," the things she really is studying are the lines of the face, the features, the walk and bearing, the shape and texture of the hand, and much besides rather than the maze of furrows and hieroglyphs in the palm, although the very manner in which one holds his hand and fingers, especially the thumb, is significant of character. Characteristic positions of the hand of course affect the lines. But it is the eyes that the gypsy watches most carefully.

In Patagonia W. H. Hudson made friends with a professional card sharp who by years of constant practice had learned to recognize the various cards of a slightly used pack by almost indistinguishable differences in wear and color. Hudson, who was himself a remarkable observer, had noticed the following phenomenon: "Gypsies are so accustomed to concentrate their sight on the eyes of the people they meet that they acquire a marvelous proficiency in detecting their expression; they study them with an object, as my friend the gambler studied the backs of cards he played with; without seeing the eyes of their intended dupe, they would be at a loss what to say." Perhaps this likewise helps to explain the peculiar penetration of the gypsy glance.

At various times I have entered gypsy fortune-telling booths incognito to study their methods. It happened that the morning of the day on which I was to be married I was pacing the streets of the Chicago Loop in a state of nervous exaltation, oblivious to my surroundings, when suddenly I found myself opposite the *ófisa* of a Nomad on South State Street, and entered it without betraying the fact I knew gypsy. Pretending I was a credulous *Gajo,* I asked the stock question, "Will I get married, and when?" Taking it for granted, therefore, that I must be in love, she claimed that if I gave her some more money she would say a charm to bring it about soon. I gave her a dime. It was not enough to satisfy her, but she muttered the charm in *Romanes,* or, as the romantic authors would say, "She uttered strange, impenetrable words of fate," which, as it turned out, were intelligible to me. Here they are: "You blankety-blank cheap skate, if you aren't more generous with your girl, I hope she gets another fellow."

When I spoke to her in gypsy she laughed, enjoying the joke as much as I had—and gave me back my money. I must admit, however, that the advice was worth more than I had given her.

Every year the laws against fortune telling become stricter. But unless mysticism and all supernatural beliefs are a crime, why should palmistry be one? A shrewd old gypsy mother, Mrs. Herne, said to me one day, "Foolish *Gajo*

girls keeps comin' to me, and I helps 'em to keep
clear of every sort o' scrape you ever fancied.
The *dŭkkerin'* I gives 'em is just the sort of
advice their mothers 'd give, but they takes it
from me—'cause they has to pay for it."

Even men of science have been known to believe in communication with spirits; and people
of education believe in predictions of the future.
Frequently Romanies have made the statement
that they would rather *dŭkker* educated persons
than illiterate ones. "They ain't so sharp," I
heard Mrs. Stanley say. "An ign'rant person
only takes *one meanin'* to a word—but they takes
four or five." Emerson has ably summed up the
entire matter in the last stanza of "The Romany
Girl."

"You doubt we read the stars on high.
  Natheless we read your fortunes true;
The stars may hide in upper sky,
  But without glass we fathom you."

The *Gajo* does not like being fathomed, and
therefore he tries to even accounts by accusing
the Romanies of being thieves. It is true that a
certain number of gypsies steal occasionally; but
so do many *Gajos,* and, unlike the latter, they
confine their practice as a rule to petty thieving,
or *čoring.* "I ain't never *čored* anything," an
Anglo-American Romani said to me, "but I've
found lots of things that weren't lost."

This is one of their many sayings in regard to the matter, and is an indication, not of hypocrisy —the homage vice pays to virtue—but of humor. Another Romani observed: "Steal? We must eat—and drink." Discussing *čoripé* one day with a French gypsy, he remarked: "We don't steal. Our women do it for us."

There is a legend among the Alsatian gypsies that when Christ was to be crucified, the Roman soldiers came to a gypsy smith and asked him to forge the four nails for the cross, one for each limb. The gypsy refused in spite of every threat, and when the nails were finally made by a Jewish smith, the gypsy tried to steal them. He only succeeded in stealing one, and that is why on the crucifix one sees both feet held by a single nail. To reward the gypsy for his most laudable efforts, the Lord has granted permission to every member of the race to steal once in seven years.

A gypsy does not steal because he is too weak to resist the temptation, but from topsy-turvy principles. Romanies feel that society has declared war on them. Being strangers and in a minority, they were persecuted from the time they first appeared in Europe. Until only little more than a hundred years ago there was a law in England making it a crime, punishable by hanging, simply to belong to their race or to speak their language. Society has opposed them with force, which they could meet only with cunning. They admire those of their number who are the craftiest, as the Greeks admired the wily Ulysses.

However, gypsies never forget a kindness shown them by *Gajos*. Walter Scott's father always let the Romanies take shelter in his barn during stormy weather. In return, they gave the son some of the most interesting episodes in *Quentin Durward*, and his greatest character, Meg Merriles.

Stevenson tells of having been refused admittance to an inn one rainy night because he was taken for a vagabond, and remarks: "It is all very fine to talk about tramps and morality. Six hours of police surveillance (such as I have had) change your views on the subject like a course of lectures. As long as you keep in the upper regions with all the world bowing to you as you go, social arrangement has a very handsome air; but once get under the wheels and you wish society at the devil. I will give most respectable men a fortnight of such a life, and then I will offer them twopence for what remains of their morality." Let us remember that the gypsies have been under the wheels for centuries.

In our own topsy-turvy way of looking at property rights, it is a greater crime to steal a chicken running by the roadside, or an ear of corn from a field, than to defraud the public of millions of dollars in natural resources. If one must steal, he should be sure to take enough to make it legal.

The Romanies have a different viewpoint. One day an Anglo-American *Romaničel* was discussing the exploits of a Serbian gypsy who had hoaxed a man of a fairly large amount. "It's folks like her as spoils this country. Make an honest livin' off the chumps; but don't steal *too much!*"

How often the pot calls the kettle black! Last year I stopped in a saloon on the edge of Cincinnati to inquire after some Nomads who had been camping in the neighborhood. They had gone, but the bartender told me an amusing incident. "They're not bad people," he remarked. "Like in every race, some's honest and some ain't. Last month a fellow come in here damnin' the gypsies and callin' 'em all a bunch of thieves. He ran out of gas up the road here by the camp, and, bein' too lazy to come down here and fetch some himself, or to send the guy that was with him, he yelled to some gypsy kids and gave them a dollar to get some. I guess they figured it was worth a dollar just to fetch it, and there wasn't no money left over to buy the gas. So they didn't think it was worth the trouble to go back. Well, he come here cussin' 'em out, and borrows a dollar off me, saying it was all the change he had and that he'd be around in the mornin' an' pay me back. I ain't seen him since."

It is a question, too, whether the gypsies are more dishonest than the persons who make capital of their sleight-of-hand propensities. A Russian who knew the Romanies intimately, Dobrowolski, relates that the nobles of central Russia often commissioned a gypsy "expert" to obtain horses for them, but always inquired in what direction it would be unsafe to ride them.

In a certain large American city I met a Nomad who announced that he was going to open an *ófisa*.

"But there's a strict city law against *drabarimus*," I said.

"What of it?" he replied. "I got a big lawyer here. Money talks. And if my wife takes too much and we get into 'trouble,' it's all fixed up in advance." He told the name of the lawyer, who was prominent in politics and society. He became district attorney, and later a judge.

We hear a great deal about graft in America, but judges and gypsies of this type are not confined to the United States. I once heard a Spanish gypsy sing the following prison song:

> " 'You say you're not a vagabond,
>   So tell us what you do!'
> 'I mostly live by stealing, Judge,
>   The same as you . . .' "

In the following case the magistrate was

merely superstitious. It was told me by a young gypsy whose family had settled down. His father had made considerable money in a legitimate gypsy profession, and, although they lived in a good house, they still spoke gypsy among themselves and maintained relations with their wilder brothers who came through the city in their wanderings. At the same time the boy studied law in the office of a well-known firm of attorneys.

"One day, a few years ago," he said to me, "some Russian gypsies I knew, who were camping just outside the town, got into trouble and, knowing I was a lawyer, they came to me to help them out. 'Tell me the truth. *Ma XoXaves! Hom Rom* (Don't lie! I'm a gypsy), and I'll do what I can.' They told me that in telling a *Gajo's* fortune one of the women had lifted a valuable jeweled pin, and the police had found it on her person." The gypsy law student looked the case up and learned that the man she had robbed was wealthy and influential. "What could I do? As my father has property here, I was able to bail her out. We knew that she wouldn't jump bail, because we were gypsies, too. It meant several years in 'stir' if I didn't do something, so I took a long chance. I took the judge aside and told him that if he sentenced the gypsy she would bring down a terrible curse on him. As I began to cite cases, frightful things

[106]

that had happened as a result of gypsy curses, I could see him growing pale. The next day her case was dismissed." The Romanies curse a great deal, and most picturesquely, but seldom as efficiently.

So great is the power of autosuggestion, and so universal the belief in the occult powers of the gypsies, that more than once their maledictions have been carried out by their victims. A friend of mine who is an eminent philosopher and psychologist, without a trace of belief in the supernatural, declared that, if he so wished, he could frighten himself to death. "As a man thinketh . . ." If this is true when the cause of the fear is known to be imaginary and subjective, what might happen in the case of a more credulous person when the cause lies wholly outside his control?

In 1916 Edward Strietback of Cincinnati changed his name, by legal proceedings in the Probate Court of Hamilton County, at the request of a stranger who had saved him from drowning in the Ohio River.

The stranger, who was then a ragged tramp, had once been a prosperous business man in another city. He had angered a gypsy, who had laid a curse upon him and told him that he would have bad luck. Although claiming not to be superstitious, he and his wife were worried. The latter died, his property burned, and his business dwindled until he was reduced to absolute poverty. The gypsy had told him that only by getting some one to take his name could the curse be removed.

Recently Strietback, who had taken the name the stranger gave him, Rex Glenwood, met the man on the streets of Cincinnati. He was well dressed and happy. His former prosperity had returned. He told the Cincinnatian that he had been looking for him because of a troubled conscience. A gypsy had said that if he could get another to take his name, the evil spell would follow that name. Strietback, then legally known as Glenwood, winced at the information; and although he claims that he is not superstitious, he immediately applied to the courts once more to secure a new name.

Probably he is less credulous than the average. Did not a certain percentage of the faculty of Harvard University admit that they were not wholly free from superstition? Some one has said that superstition is the poetry of popular belief.

Many a Romani in America has grown rich on the gullibility of the *Gajo*. A wealthy Chicagoan who rents "concessions" told me that his agent was approached by some gypsies who wanted to use a corner of his shooting galleries for a fortune-telling booth on State Street. The Romanies were ragged and claimed to be poor.

Twenty-five dollars a week was all they could pay. As there were complaints about them, the agent raised the rent to fifty dollars in order to be rid of them. They stayed. He then raised it to one hundred; but they paid it, still maintaining they were poor. Even though it finally went to a hundred and fifty dollars a week, they remained—and prospered.

Frequently they rent a doorway and live in the rooms above, or a store, and curtain off the front as an *ófisa,* and live in the rear. I have seen as many as six large families living thus in one flat. Sitting behind the curtains, one often hears amusing things which they tell the *Gajos.* Since nearly all Romanies deplore the practice of *XoXano,* or downright cheating, because it has "spoiled the country," making it increasingly difficult to obtain a fortune teller's license, I feel it is no breach of faith to tell a few of the tricks.

One morning I was squatting on the floor of such an establishment on the West Side of Chicago. A *čei* came to me with a newspaper and asked me to read the names of the horses entered in the next day's race in Havana. She repeated the unfamiliar names with the utmost ease. In passing let me say that gypsies' memories are prodigious. In India the gypsies are often keepers of pedigrees for the aristocracy, because of their extraordinary faculties of retention. In telling the story of my Romani ances-

try to an Anglo-American, I once contradicted a
detail I had told two years before. With a
gentle smile she remarked, by way of a hint: "A
man as wants to make a good liar 'as got to 'ave
a long mem'ry, ain't he?" And now to return to
the *čei*. From behind the curtain I heard her
giving tips on the races to the people who came
for a "reading."

Rehearsing a spell in tones that were really
awe-inspiring, she invoked the spirits to pick a
winner. I shall not give all the incantation, even
in Romani. It is a tongue in which no words are
taboo. The language of the most chaste is
franker than even Rabelais. Any chance gypsy
who might read this would not be shocked, but
there are a few *Gajos* who would understand.
One of the mildest expressions was: *"Nai gogi-
aver. Mutres-pes ando taXtai, t'ai pies les
kulesa, gajikanes."* The group with which I was
sitting greeted this solemn spell with suppressed
chuckles. The spirits were evidently in a fickle
mood, for they continued to pick a different winner for each *Gajo* until all the nine entries for
that particular race were exhausted.

Only one of the nine *Gajos* returned; but that
one came back very much excited. "How did
you know? The guys said I was nuts to back
that horse—an eighteen-to-one shot. I kissed me
five bucks good-by."

"Spirits, she know lot. You give me one hundred dollar. I play for you. You make one thousand."

"Geez! that's easy money!" he remarked, handing her the ninety dollars he had won. Easy money, indeed, but not for him, since he never saw it again. As playing the races is against the law, I doubt if he mentioned the matter to the police.

The commonest trick is that of putting money in a handkerchief, which is then blessed so that the money will be increased. When the dupe opens the handkerchief a week later according to instructions, he finds some worthless paper; and when he returns to the camp or *ófisa,* he finds that the witch who blessed it has vanished into thin air.

An up-to-date variety of this type of *XoXano* was practiced by a Hungarian gypsy I knew casually in Pennsylvania, and who is now in a federal penitentiary. He invented a machine for making money, just the sort of thing to appeal to people of the Mechanical Age. One had only to insert a dollar bill in the machine, turn the crank —and out came two bills. They were brand-new United States Treasury notes, not counterfeit.

The owner of a delicatessen store in Pittsburgh, who was about to purchase the machine for a huge sum, took care to verify the fact that they were genuine; and in so doing he aroused the curiosity of a government agent, who succeeded in locating the gypsy and his machine. He found that the contrivance was indeed capable of making money—for the gypsy. As he took the latter into custody, just before the sale of the money box, the gypsy pleaded naïvely with the officer to let him go, because, in spite of the arrest, the owner of the delicatessen still believed in the machine.

Recently a detective in plain clothes entered a "phrenology" booth in Chicago to ascertain if the gypsy proprietress was really a scientific phrenologist. Feeling a bump on his head where he had been blackjacked, she said: "This bump, bump of fight. You have loss of money soon. But you good sport." The reading proved scientifically correct except for the last detail. When the detective found that he had sustained a loss of six dollars during the reading, he arrested the prophetess.

In 1921 a series of incidents occurred in Cincinnati which attracted wide attention, but the entire story has never before been pieced together. A grocer from one of the Balkan countries, who had a store on Central Avenue, Nick Stamina, had a serious misfortune. He shot a man. The fellow was an honest Serbian workman who owed Stamina a considerable sum for groceries. Owing to sickness in his family, the Serbian was unable to pay for several months, and some ill-advised friend told the grocer that he was planning to leave town and not pay his bill. Stamina therefore brought legal proceedings against him. All the fellow's furniture was sold for debt and his family put out on the street.

This action so roused the Serbians of the community that they threatened to put the "Serbian curse" on Stamina, who, being timid and superstitious, was frightened by both the curse and apprehension of physical revenge. One day the Serbian entered his store and reached for his hip pocket. Prepared for violence, Stamina seized a revolver and fired. The poor man sank to the floor in a pool of blood. He had reached for a wallet in his trousers pocket in order to pay the bill.

The Serbian curse had proved effective. The grocer was arrested, charged with assault with intent to kill, and bound over to the grand jury under heavy bonds. The incident preyed on his mind.

That spring a great many gypsies came to Cincinnati. I had never seen so many in the city before. There were numerous *ófisas* in the foreign section, and camps in the surrounding country. All had automobiles. There was one *Romano platso* in the hills above Mill Creek Valley, which sheltered as wild a crew as I have ever met. It was a beautiful situation in a clump of huge silver beeches. The ground on which the tents were pitched was covered with violets and

anemones. After talking with the chief and a
horde of curious Romainies, I noticed a woman in
a tent standing apart from the others. She
beckoned to me, and I entered the tent. In a
corner lay a young boy with blond hair, and a
vacant look in his blue eyes. *"Dilo si? Pen-ta
mandi, kai nai dilo!"* she said in agonized tones.
("Is he insane? Tell me he isn't!") The boy
was clearly an imbecile. "Give us bread; we are
hungry!" she pleaded. I inquired and learned
that some years before, she had given herself to
a *Gajo.* Feeling that she was sufficiently punished by having a half-witted *Gajo* child, the
gypsies had not banished her from the tribe, but
had forced her to live somewhat apart and shift
for herself for a certain number of years.

When I left I was taken to the street-car line
in a broken-down Ford. It was falling apart
with rust. The floor was completely gone. A
dozen Romanies, young and old, climbed in or
held on by some means or other. The car managed to reach the bottom of the hill. But I doubt
if it ever reached the top again.

Not all the gypsies were half-witted, and all
did not ride in Fords. Far from it! There were
two families that had taken quarters in vacant
stores on Central Avenue, whose members were
among the cleverest I have ever met. One of
these Romanies, Pete Yuno, was a young fellow,
twenty-two or twenty-three, but he owned an

expensive high-powered motor car, and was famous for his ability as a rapid, accurate driver. *"Tradel mišto mobilesa,"* the others said of him. His wife was far from pretty, but there was all of the wisdom and fascinating powers of the serpent in her dark, beady eyes.

Pete's *ófisa* was near Nick Stamina's grocery, and it was not long before he heard of the latter's plight and offered to help him. He was a Serbian gypsy; and who could be better qualified to lift the "Serbian curse" from Stamina's head? No easy task, nor one that could be done in a moment! There were many spirits to be propitiated.

In the dim basement, underneath the very spot where the Serbian's blood had stained the floor, sacrifices were made to the gods of destruction by squeezing red juice from a bushel of beets. Since money had been the root of the trouble, the evil god of money, a distinctly modern deity, was placated by burning a dollar bill. Other ceremonies of the black art were performed at intervals for some months, during which time Pete and his wife, Yano, had won the complete confidence of the grocer by their refusal to accept payment for their valuable services. Also the plain but fascinating Yano had charmed not only the gods, but also the grocer.

One beautiful morning a few months later I

started for the country to visit the gypsies. The camp had taken French leave. There was nothing surprising about this; but when I went from place to place and found that, of all the different tribes and families, not one remained, I was puzzled. Not for long, however, for I overheard some one in the street say: "Can you imagine anyone being such a saphead? Seven thousand dollars!" The morning paper explained it all.

Pete and Yano had persuaded the grocer that as the spirits were not wholly conciliated, he must get together all the wealth he had, some seven thousand dollars and jewelry, and carry it on his person for a day. But even this proved unavailing. As the gypsies had more power over the gods, they must carry the money. Naturally, Stamina kept a close watch on them. Still the gods were angry. It was then decided that the grocer must make a pilgrimage to Dayton that day. A boy was left to keep an eye on the Romanies, who still carried the treasure.

In a minute or two, while the boy was not watching, the gypsies' things were packed in the car and they were in their seats. The boy jumped on the running board, protesting, but a gentle push of the foot sent him sprawling on his back. When he arose they had vanished.

On his return Stamina loudly bewailed the disappearance of Yano and his ducats. He had lost his money and felt convinced that the spells were all a lie. He still faced a long confinement in the penitentiary. But if he thought that the curse had not been removed, he was mistaken. On the dreaded day of his trial for assault with intent to kill, the wise and kind-hearted judge declared that it was obvious that Stamina was a man of better intentions than judgment, and that he had already been punished sufficiently for his rashness by the loss of his property through the gypsies. To his surprise and joy he was set completely free.

The spirits, however, still demanded their pound of flesh. The curse passed from his head to that of the gypsies. Some unregenerate Romani had demanded a certain sum for keeping silent, an unheard-of proceeding. Yano had refused to pay it, and in consequence the police were informed, according to Troka, a gypsy acquaintance of mine, though of course the detectives took the entire credit to themselves. Yano and Pete were arrested in Michigan, brought back, tried, and sentenced to a long term in jail, in spite of the fact that they had fulfilled their contract with the grocer by removing the Serbian curse.

One of the latest methods of evading the law, bootlegging, is seldom practiced by gypsies; but recently, meeting Kolya in a large mid-Western city, he asked me if I had seen an old friend of mine, Fantaco. "Fantaco is rich now. One week ago he buy automobile for sixteen thousand dollars." He had bought a drug store, including the druggist. Some of the Romanies are being Americanized with startling rapidity.

Many gypsies have a remarkably good knowledge of medicinal plants and their curative powers. Herb-doctoring is one of their most ancient and characteristic professions. They do not always take the trouble, however, to prepare actual medicines. One day I was sitting behind the scenes with some Romanies, when a man entered and was taken aside by one of the women. He was being treated for a liver complaint. "I'm feeling much better," he remarked with a faint groan, "but I'd like some more of that pink medicine. It helped me more than the blue." When he had gone, I learned that both were pure water with the addition of harmless coloring water. For centuries they have been obtaining cures by means of autosuggestion. The laugh which we all had, after the man had left, was worth more to the gypsies than the fee they had charged.

After all is said and done, the gypsy is a lovable rogue; and if he cheats occasionally it is partly to even the score with his ancient enemy, the *Gajo,* but chiefly for the fun of it. If they beg, it is with such consummate art, and if they deceive, it is so good-naturedly that the victim cannot complain. I remember a Yankee horse-dealer saying to a gypsy: "I like you, Nick; you always get the best of me—but you do it so damned slick." They do it with a love of the game for its own sake. As one of them said to another, "He'd steal his own hat, just to have a laugh."

Watching a game of cards one night in a cross-roads saloon opposite an Anglo - American Romani camp in Wisconsin, I noticed that the two gypsies who were playing partners against two *Gajos* were cheating. When one of their opponents finally became aware of this, the Romanies burst into such loud, unfeigned laughter that the men who were being fooled were completely disarmed, and, hardened horse-traders though they were, with a heavy coat of tan, they both blushed, and were forced to join in the merriment.

Of the many false ideas in regard to this delightful, wayward race, the falsest and most pernicious is that they steal children. There are various reasons for the existence of this belief, though there is not a single well-authenticated case of kidnapping by gypsies. It doubtless sprang up spontaneously in various lands as a means of frightening children into being "good." The harm to children's minds has been great, and the harm done to the gypsies even greater.

Another reason for the prevalence of this belief is the fact that there have been so many

stories with kidnapping as the principal device
for securing a happy ending. The heroine turns
out to be not a despised gypsy, after all, but the
stolen daughter of the forlorn mother, or of the
noble lady. An early playwright of Seville,
Lope de Rueda, was probably the first author to
hit on this clever artifice; but Cervantes best developed it in *The Little Gypsy Girl,* and since
then the imitators of his imitators have been
countless.

The moment a child disappears for any reason,
all gypsy camps are immediately ransacked by a
sheriff's posse; and so high does feeling run on
such occasions, that the mob sometimes does violence to the Romanies on mere groundless suspicion. Such is the emotional effect of the crime
of kidnapping, that the mere thought of it causes
men to act most irrationally. I have investigated
numerous cases of alleged child stealing, and now
and again I have been puzzled momentarily.
Not long ago I read the following headlines:
"King of gypsies says Glass boy is in Argentina.
John Cruse declares kidnapped child is held by
band," but the article contained the following
words, "Both Cruse and his wife, 'Queen Maria,'
deny any knowledge of the whereabouts of
Jimmy Glass."

Often runaway children try to excuse themselves to their parents by saying they were seized
by gypsies; and such is the fascination of the

Romanies over the minds of certain children—
as well as grown-ups—that they are sometimes
besieged with pleas to take them along, pleas to
which the wanderers turn a deaf ear for many
reasons.

But the cases which puzzled me most were
cases where young gypsy girls, almost invariably
married ones, had run away from their tribe and
claimed to the *Gajos* that they had been kidnapped in their childhood. The motives have
been a quarrel with the boy husband, with
whom they were not truly in love, or with
parents, the desire to cause a stir and be talked
about, and the love of hoaxing the *Gajos*. Playing thus on the romantic imaginations and sym-
pathies of the non-gypsies, more than one
Romani lass in this country has taken up a large
collection in order to return to some distant place
to parents that never existed.

There are many variations to this phenomenon
of *čei našli*, or runaway gypsy girl. In one instance the child first claimed she had been sold in
marriage by non-gypsy parents. It is possible
that she had not been kindly treated. Perhaps,
too, there was a strain of *Gajo* blood in her veins
and the call of civilization was too much for her.
The Romani mother offered to give her child
money, gypsy finery, and jewelry; and when
every effort to win her back had failed, she fell
to the ground in front of the court house, where

she had waited all day in vain for a glimpse of her. The frantic wails of the mother were heard for blocks. In the days that followed she wandered the streets, telling her trouble to those she met: "They put her in school, like jail. Look at my lips. They are all dry. I no eat for wanting my girl. I kill myself. I kill myself."

Another case of *čei našli,* in which I happened to know the principals, was that of one of the Mitchell girls who ran away and married a boy in another band of gypsies. Quarreling with her mate, she returned to her father. As the latter had not received the customary sum for the marriage of his daughter, he was angry with the groom and his parents, and in order to make trouble for them he claimed his daughter had been kidnapped. Needless to say, he did not reveal to the police the fact that he and his daughter were also Romanies.

What motive would the gypsies have for kidnapping non-gypsy children? Their dislike for those who are not of the same blood as themselves amounts in many cases to positive disgust. There are many Romanies who will not sleep in a bed that a *Gajo* has slept in, or drink from a glass that one of them has ever touched. It is true that they are fond of children, fonder, in fact, than of life itself—but they always have plenty of their own.

CHAPTER V

NOMADS OF FIELD AND SLUM

JOYS of the open road! Joys of wandering over level plains, of following the wind, of going and going across wide grassy seas, end without end, with no horizon walls but the great blue sky! Joys of scaling the giant rock-ribbed peaks, of roaming fields of everlasting snow, of standing on lofty summits and thrilling to the wonder-striking sight of awesome gulfs, chain on chain of white crests like angry waves and on every side the spread of infinite space!

But where is the mountain that does not rise from an abyss, and where is the joy in roaming that does not entail hardships? How could I love the vast white silences if I did not love the teeming cities? How could I worship solitude if I had not known the joys of plunging in the tides of humanity? In cities one may be as much alone as in the desert, or one may find companions by the score. The veriest wreck of a human being is worth more than oceans of inert matter. Nature is only a mirror in which one sees the many facets of one's inner soul, but to transcend self one needs the aid of man.

The wanderlust was on me that summer, and, not being able to satisfy it otherwise, I had jumped on a moving freight that came puffing through the dusk near Lake Monona, and, slowly gathering momentum, had gone crashing through the darkness. Night after night I had lain awake and listened to the call of the engine whistles in the stillness. Each had its own message to my trained ear: the proud passenger locomotive, the gossipy switch engine, the determined freight engine with the slow huf-huf of its breath coming faster and faster till it faded in the distance—but all of them cried to me to come.

After two weeks of riding the rods, head ends, and coal cars, known on the road as gondolas; of fraternizing with tramps in "jungles," and sleeping in ten-cent "flops"—I probably did not present a very prosperous appearance. The whim of a capricious "rattler," bound I knew not whither, had taken me to Chicago, and habit and my own feet had brought me to Halsted Street. And there in front of a shooting gallery I saw a beautiful gypsy girl with a rose in her hair, hailing the passers-by to come and have their fortunes told. Her costume was most picturesque, almost operatic, but different from that of the Nomads. I spoke to her in Romani, and was rewarded with a smile such as only a gypsy can give. She called to a younger brother, a fourteen-year-old boy, who greeted me cordially and suggested a stroll.

We had scarcely gone ten steps when, without preliminaries, he said, as he eyed my trampish exterior: "Brother, I'll give you all I have. It isn't much, but I have a large camera I can pawn if you like." Life in the trenches and on the road breeds a comradeship which is worth any amount of hardship, but there is nothing like the friendship of gypsies.

This was my first introduction to Rumanian Romanies, the "Bear-folki," who bear an evil reputation among Anglo - American gypsies which is wholly undeserved.

The following autumn a traveling carnival came to Madison. I was there on the grounds soon after it arrived, in hopes of finding Romanies. Not finding any at first, I was leaving in disappointment, when, as I passed the last tent, a wild-animal show, I heard a half-familiar voice cry out, "Roma!" It was Karol, the boy who had offered to pawn his camera.

We were both delighted to meet again so soon. Observing that I was better dressed than on the previous occasion, he remarked, "You have had luck since I saw you, *prala.* Come and meet the rest of the family, my older brother, my father, and Bill." His father, Sando, a short, powerfully built gypsy, stood in the sawdust ring,

[125]

cracking a long whip and shouting to a pony in *Romanes*. He was teaching it to do tricks. Sando was an extraordinary combination of sternness and kindliness, like a steel watch spring, both firm and gently yielding. His eyes could blaze with a fierce hypnotic light that held one numb, or they could beam with a warm tenderness.

The brother, Mario, dressed like a cowboy, was tall and good-looking. He was training an enormous bear. After being introduced to the father and son, I asked: "Where is the rest of the family? You spoke of Bill."

"Oh," he replied, "Bill's the bear." I had no desire, however, to shake hands with him. Mario was teaching him a new wrestling hold, and as they stood locked in one another's embrace, his shaggy muzzle, with a ring in his nose, projected above the former's head. The man was treating him roughly, digging a diamond into his side and teasing him. Bill resented the treatment and growled threateningly.

Suddenly Mario's face went white and he gasped. The father jumped to his side and gave a sharp command. The bear was crushing him in his paws. At the word from Sando the beast relaxed its grip, and both the son and the bear stood with hanging heads, looking sheepish. "How many times have I told you not to tease him?" he shouted at the former. "And as for you . . ." He turned to the animal and stung it with his lash. The animal winced with pain, but showed no signs of resentment against this display of paternal authority. Its large eyes seemed to say: "It's a father's right. I was just giving a brotherly hug, but Mario had better be careful or . . ." I shuddered to think what might happen some day if Sando were absent.

Bill had been caught in the Alps by the gypsies, and had learned a number of tricks, but he was still as essentially wild as any Romani.

"Let's have a swim," Karol suggested. Permission was obtained from the father, and we started off: the two brothers, a pet monkey on Karol's shoulder, and myself. We went to a spot beyond where the Yahara flows out of Mendota, and, undressing in a clump of willow slips, we plunged into the clear lake. The gypsies swam like trout, laughing, and splashing the water in crystal showers. Overhead, the monkey swung like a pendulum from a long willow branch, enjoying the fun.

As they stepped out on the bank their brown bodies, lithe and strong, glistening in the September sun, were as beautiful as the polished bronze statues of the ancient gods.

"Where in hell are my clothes?" exclaimed Mario, as he searched in vain through the bushes. "Some —— —— *Gajo* has swiped them, I'll bet." It was an embarrassing plight even for a gypsy. Looking overhead for the monkey, he saw them neatly hidden in the fork of a large tree.

In order to repay Karol for the kindness he had shown me on our first meeting, I wrote an article for one of the papers, describing the animal show at the carnival in glowing terms, mentioning the fact that the owners were gypsies and urging everyone to attend.

The following evening I entered the grounds. The canvas inclosure was a flare of light and color from gasoline torches and lurid posters. There was a mingled odor of roasting peanuts, wild beasts, humanity, and fragrant pine sawdust. One could hear the shout of the "barkers" drawing the crowd to The Old Plantation Singers, The Den of Freaks, .The Turkish Harem, and above their cries the piercing nasal notes of the Oriental flute in the hootchi-kootchi, the murmur of the crowd, and the click of the wheels of fortune.

In front of the animal show Mario was doing the barking, and Karol selling tickets. I bought one and went inside. A fairly large crowd gathered, but to my surprise there were few women and children, though the latter would have enjoyed it immensely. When the performance was about to begin, Karol passed me and slipped the quarter I had paid into my pocket.

Various animals did a number of clever things,

but the drawing card was the bear. He roller-
skated and danced to a tango, while Sando sang
in Spanish to the accompaniment of a tam-
bourine. Next, Mario wrestled with the bear
and threw him, while the father directed the
movements of Bill in Romani.

Sando then announced that he would give
twenty-five dollars to anyone who could throw
the bear, and assured the crowd that it was
properly muzzled, tame, and held to the rules of
either Greco-Roman or catch-as-catch-can, and
that undue hugging was barred. The crowd was
all agog, but at first no one would try his skill.
Finally a burly negro flung off his coat and
struggled to put Bill four points down. The
fellow's strength piqued the bear's pride and he
was about to fling the negro to the ground, when
a word from Sando in gypsy restrained him and
he "threw the fight." This was merely by way
of advertisement, since the bear could easily have
beaten his opponent. A number of others tried
to win the twenty-five dollars, but all were
downed by the animal at Sando's pleasure.

When the show was over I stepped up to the
father and mentioned the article I had written to
draw the crowd. His expression changed in a
flash from one of benevolence to anger. "Was it
you?" he cried. *"Dilo!* You're crazy. Why, you
say we are gypsies! No mother bring her child
here, for fear we kidnap it." With that he

turned on his heel. I walked away very much crestfallen. I had tried to do a kindness and had harmed my friends. Karol followed me. "Never mind *o dat*," he said, trying to comfort me. "He's cross sometimes, but he's good to us."

Here is a typical instance of the harm done by the ridiculous idea that gypsies steal children.

The number of Rumanian gypsies in America is relatively small, although Rumania has the largest percentage of gypsies of any country. One out of every thirty of the inhabitants is a Romani. Partly because of their numbers, partly because of former laws enslaving gypsies, most of the gypsies in that country are settled, and very much Gajified, like those of Seville. Exceptions are the semisavage, thieving *netosi* and the *ursari,* or bear leaders, to which class my friends belonged. Numerous are the amusing adventures I have had among Romanies of every type in Rumania, but none have been more enjoyable than my experience with Karol and his brothers, in spite of the unfortunate outcome.

Many of the Rumanian *Roms* have completely forgotten their tongue; and those in this country speak it very imperfectly. Their dress, too, is usually *Gajikano*—either American or Rumanian. But they have one thing which has survived all changes—their jewelry. I have met a number of them, in various parts of the United States, whom one would have taken for non-

gypsies were it not for their magnificent bracelets, necklaces, and amulets of ancient Oriental
make, exactly like those of the Nomads.

Not only does one find gypsy blood among
the pleasure-loving boyars, or grandees, of the
Balkan country, more than one of whom has had
a romance with the *vatrasi,* or gypsy house ser-
vants; but one also finds many "aficionados," or
gypsified *Gajos.*

One of the latter is the well-known Romany
Marie, whose father was a tavern-keeper in
Rumania. With her husband, she keeps one of
the most interesting cafés of New York's
Bohemia, Greenwich Village. On the walls are
odd pictures, posters, and examples of native
handicrafts. Not only is the place itself attractive, but the habitués are even more so, with the
exception of "uptown slummers." Most interesting of all is Romany Marie herself. A former
artist's model and a friend and adviser to many
a young girl who has come to New York to tread
the long and thorny road of art, she is also a
friend to the gypsies, and more than once she has
answered the call of the road. Sitting one evening in the dim café, enjoying a tasty Rumanian
dish and listening to a record of gypsy music, we
discussed artists and Romanies. "After all," she
remarked, "they are very much alike."

It was Murger who coined the term Bohemian,

in his famous *Vie de Bohême*. It is simply the French word for gypsy—*Bohémien*.

The fall I met the "bear-folki" I suffered more than ever from the nostalgia for roaming. When Christmas vacation came and most of my fellow undergraduates left the city, it was almost intolerable. Seated late one night in a corner of the former Bismarck, sampling a glass of dark Münchener with another student, I suddenly proposed that we go to Chicago.

"How can we," he answered, "if we have only seven dollars between us? It wouldn't pay our fares there and back."

"Never mind. We won't pay any fares."

There was a fast express train leaving at three o'clock that morning. It made only one stop between Madison and Chicago, and we counted on arriving before being frozen to death. Just as it was pulling out of the station we swung aboard the "blind," the front end of the baggage car, which is never opened, for fear of train robbers. There is a ledge about a foot wide on which we sat with legs dangling over the dizzily whizzing space between our car and the tender, as the train attained a speed of some sixty miles an hour.

It was bitterly cold. Fearing we might be numbed and slip from our precarious perch, we climbed up the side of the tender, and lay on lumps of soft coal on top of the steel water tank. I wish the person who first called bituminous coal

Necklaces and bracelets are very popular and of many forms. Some of them are extremely ancient and valuable

"soft" might lie on some jagged lumps of it on a swaying, bouncing locomotive. I am sure he would find a more descriptive term.

The smoke from the engine trailed above us in a long straight line, illuminated by the red glow from the open fire box. There is nothing more infernal than the gray and scarlet billows, roaring, twisting, and shooting at a terrific velocity over your head, while you plunge through the night in the midst of a deafening din. And I know of few things more thrilling.

At Janesville we stopped for water, and a kindly fireman, who doubtless felt we had earned our ride, merely remarked, "Kind o' cold, ain't it?" as he came back to adjust the pipe. Suddenly a liquid stream, a foot or two in diameter, shot from above into the tank where we were, wetting us with its icy spray. Fortunately the lumps of coal on which we were lying saved us from being soaked to the skin and freezing to the steel.

To make matters worse, it began to snow. A tornado can blow a straw through trees and plate glass, and the speed of the wind, added to that of the express, made the sharp flakes strike our faces like needles.

It was twilight as we entered the city. As the train did not slacken its pace, the horrible thought came to us that we might be carried into the station and ignominiously hauled from our

places by the police and given another free ride
—to the lock-up.

Fortunately, a little later it slowed down
enough to enable us to jump to the ground. At
this point the tracks were on a concrete elevation
with smooth walls about the height of a second-
story window. How were we going to reach the
ground? Finally, after walking half a mile down
the track we saw a snowbank below, and, trusting
to luck that it contained nothing hard, we leaped
off and alighted unhurt.

My companion was not exactly in a singing
mood, but to pluck up spirits he managed to
chant in a plaintive voice:

> " 'Where do we go from here, boys?
> Where do we go from here?' "

When I replied we would take refuge in the
house of some gypsy or other, he was not particularly reassured.

After a long tramp, half frozen, and worn out
from lack of sleep, we finally found a house in
the Maxwell Street district which was inhabited
by two families of Nomads, those of Koina and
Išvan, whom I had never met before. They
were cordial enough with me, but they eyed my
Gajo friend askance. It was true that I had
broken a Romani custom in asking shelter for a
non-gypsy. As the saying goes: *"Rom romesa,*

Gajo Gajesa ("Gypsy with gypsy, Gentile with Gentile").

We told something of our plight, taking care not to mention that we were students. Naturally they were puzzled at two well-dressed young men having chosen to ride the "blind" in such weather. With the politeness and dignity of the gentleman and the true gypsy the world over, Koina made no comment, forbearing to question us further. One of the boys, however, went through the pantomime of blowing a safe, and then grinned from ear to ear. The fact that they believed we were bandits did not keep them from offering hospitality, but it created a dangerous situation for ourselves, in spite of the fact that they believed I was gypsy.

We were shown to a small room off the large one, containing the one bed in the establishment, and were given thick eiderdown quilts to lie between. We took off our coats and shoes and, pulling the quilts well up around our heads, we were as "snug as a bug in a rug." In justice to the gypsies be it said that we were the *only* bugs in the bed. Our last seven dollars were in the pocket of my coat, hanging on the wall beside the bed. I did not remove the money in front of Koina, in order not to hurt his feelings; and, once we were in bed and had closed the door, I dismissed all thought of transferring it to my person as an insult to the gypsy race.

Although we were dead tired, it was not easy to go to sleep. Koina's wife, Nura, had set aside the morning for mourning. At given intervals the Nomads and Coppersmith gypsies celebrate festivals for the dead, wailing at the grave, pouring libations upon it, and holding funeral feasts. Some time before, Nura's father had died. As the grave was in another country, she could only withdraw behind a curtain with a bottle of brandy, pull a shawl over her head, and pour the libations in herself. They helped her to release her very genuine and poignant feelings, and to wail with greater intensity.

I have lain awake under the stars in the Snake River Cañon, near Idaho, and listened to the blood-curdling howl of the gentle prairie wolves, and I have heard the hunger cry of the tiger resounding through the night; but there are notes in the human voice which are more lugubrious, more unnerving. Of such were the groans and direful wails of Nura lamenting the dead.

Suddenly the sound of a quarrel between Išvan and Koina reached our ears, but so muffled that it was impossible to hear what it was about. A little later there was a sound of naked feet scurrying across the floor, followed by the crash of a breaking window. And dominating all these noises came the unceasing cries of Nura: *"Devla! Devla! Devla!"* ("God! O God! O God!")

But so sleepy was I, that in spite of all I fell

into a doze, only to awaken when I felt the elbow of my companion prodding me in the ribs. Opening my eyes, I saw his blanched face turned in the direction of the wall, where Koina was going through his pockets.

I have never had any apprehension from gypsies who regarded me as one of them. I have never received the dreaded wooden ring which summons one to secret trial by night. I have never had a Romani wear the death shirt for me, the symbol that gives the right to kill without further notice. It is true that a Giano drew a knife against me, but he did not believe I was one of the blood. It is true also that I have been assaulted by *Gajos* while looking for gypsies, for the class of Gentiles among whom one finds them is often dangerous. But here was a new peril: I had chosen a *Gajo* for a companion, and among the deepest, wildest Romanies the *Gajo* is legitimate prey. Furthermore, we were in a tough district, the men were obviously poor, perhaps hungry, and in their belief the stakes were large.

Koina, however, proved to be a genuine *Rom*. After making a thorough search in my companion's coat, he left without touching mine. Sleep was out of the question. A little later we arose and took our leave. I bought a beefsteak and brought it back, for Sebenca, Išvan's wife, to cook for us all; but after that nothing would induce my friend to return, which was doubtless wise.

There was a period in my life when love of travel took the form of hoboing, "beating my way," the malady known to tramps as "railroad fever." My first experience, at the age of fifteen, came near being my last, in fact my last experience of any kind whatsoever.

Like every American boy, I had a passion for Indians—and still have, for that matter. There was old Indian John, who camped near Madison and made me a hickory bow in my childhood; and there was Jane, a buxom Nez Percé, whom I met in a wigwam in the West and with whom I almost fell in love at the age of seventeen, when she tied a string of beads about my wrist with plump but, oh, such deft fingers, and for whose sake I tried to acquire a taste for the sun-dried eels her father used to spear in the Snake River. Indians, individually, collectively, and historically, have always been a passion with me, though nothing like my passion for gypsies.

I had played as a child in the cave which, according to legend, had been the hiding place for Black Hawk, one of the noblest and most pathetic figures in the history of the redskins; and my father had discovered the exact site of his last battle with the whites, a valley on the banks of the Wisconsin River. There I determined to go one morning late in March, and "hopped freight" bound for Maizomanie.

The only car where I would be hidden from the brakemen was a flat car loaded with lumber and two veteran hobos, "blowed-in-the-glass stiffs," the kind who make it a principle of honor never to work except in chain gangs, and never to pay tribute to the "shacks," the brakemen, who often accept bribes for the privilege of riding unmolested. "Where you bound, Jack?" asked one. "It's getting chilly," remarked the other, handing me a flash of rot-gut whisky with the comradery of the road. "Last night I slept on a grave in the cemetery, with the tombstone for a pillow," said the first. "I need something to limber me up." Half the contents of the pint flask disappeared in prolonged gulps.

Later, as we bowled along with a clatter that made conversation impossible, a burly shack suddenly appeared and demanded: "Fork over! Pay yer fares!" He was greeted with derisive oaths and cries of, "Come and get it!"

"I'll get *youse,* you lousy bums!" he retorted, and sprang from the box car to the pile of lumber where we were sitting. The prospect of a free-for-all fight on such unstable footing, where a misstep meant death, was not to my taste. As one of the hobos made a movement toward his razor pocket, however, the brakeman decided to retreat, after promising to eat our white livers raw for breakfast.

As the train began to slow down, I climbed to the forward end of the car, in readiness to jump. The sudden clamping of the brakes pitched me headlong, and it was only with a terrific wrench that I managed to seize a rod on the next car and keep from falling between the wheels.

I saw my battlefield, however, from the high hill where Black Hawk had directed his men. The wide river, swollen by spring freshets, and the long vista of pine bluffs, as wild and desolate as the day of the battle, were wonderfully impressive.

Since then, I had often "bummed my way" about the country, "jungling up" with tramps and listening to many a strange story by their camp fires. There was a thrill to this roving life that was lacking in the conventional modes of travel which my parents generously provided. The tramps themselves were not without interest. There is something of the artist and philosopher in the hobo. His attitude toward life is non-utilitarian and æsthetic, though he is far from an æsthetic object himself. One of the most interesting debates to which I have ever listened was a discussion on the freedom of the will, which I heard in a ten-cent "flop."

There is an atmosphere of moral decay among them, however, which distinguishes them from the gypsies. The tramps are mostly mere wrecks of men, pathological cases, sterile offshoots, lacking the robust, sunny humanity of the Romanies. I was fascinated by hoboing, and horrified by the fascination—like a man descending a damp, railingless stairway in the darkness above a bottomless pit, fearful lest he fall, yet half attracted by the gulf.

The spring after my escapade in Chicago I listened with unheeding ears to the call of the engine whistles; but when summer came I was off on the road again, singing at the top of my lungs as I stood in a "gondola," whirling down the tracks beside the Mississippi. At Dubuque I waited all day with a hobo to catch a freight. Nothing passed us but trains of sealed box cars. Finally, tired of waiting, my companion called out, "So long!" and, as one of the cars passed at high speed, he made a running dive, and plunged beneath it, landing unhurt on the rods. That night, finding an open box car, known to the 'bos as a side-door Pullman, I lay down to sleep. I awoke to find that two of the toughest-looking specimens of the human animal that I have ever seen had climbed in somewhere along the line. They demanded money, but, as I denied having any and put on a bold front, they let me alone. Most tramps are "lost-nerves," with more bluff in them than fight.

Nevertheless, I got out at the next stop and

climbed on the front of the locomotive of a passenger train that happened to come along. Riding the "head end," perched above the cow catcher, is more exhilarating than even tobogganing or ice-boating. It was a through express, and we bored the darkness at a fearful pace. Gradually the dawn arose across the Illinois prairie, and we raced eastward straight into a dazzling sunrise, more beautiful even than any I have seen in the Alps.

If all roads lead to Rome, all railroads lead to Chicago, and there I found myself two days later. I had a ten-dollar bill sewed into the lining of my flannel shirt, as a reserve; but, as the June night was mild, I decided to "carry the banner" —walk the streets instead of sleeping in a lodging house.

After midnight, too sleepy to walk any farther, I went to Grant Park beside the Lake and lay down. Above me rose the shadow of the tall buildings on Michigan Boulevard, outlined against the velvety blue of the star-filled sky, like a great cliff. When I awoke the sun was still behind the water's edge, which was hidden by a pale mist. It was impossible to tell where the Lake left off and the sky began—a sweep of infinite gray. Gradually it began to glow with a coppery flame, and showers of gleaming sparks danced on the broad surface of the waters. The sun had risen.

All around me lay the black forms of hundreds of sleeping tramps. Their inert bodies gave the impression of a battlefield strewn with corpses.

As the ground was moist with dew, I continued my nap on a bench on the Boulevard, opposite the Annex Hotel, where just a year before I had spent a joyous evening in the Pompeian Room, the world's most luxurious café, with a corps of drink mixers, each an artist, specializing in some particular combination. The last few days I had been living on the beans and stews served in the hang-outs with a nickel glass of beer the size of a bucket. I was dreaming, therefore, of the dainty free lunches prepared by a famous French chef in the Pompeian Room, when a policeman stung the soles of my feet with a smart blow of his club.

Michigan Boulevard is unique, but personally I have always found Halsted Street more entertaining; and, as the "Boul Mich" was not in a hospitable mood, I started for Halsted. The latter is not only the longest, but is also the most cosmopolitan, street on the entire globe. It is more foreign than "abroad." As New York is overcrowded with immigrants, the newer arrivals flock to Chicago, and, in order not to be swamped by the tides of alien life about them, each group clings to its national customs with a tenacity unknown in their native land.

In Naples I searched for days for theaters

which still maintained the old comedies of masks; and I only discovered one, which gave but one play a week. In Halsted Street I found two rival theaters with Pulcinellas, the ancestor of Punch and Pierrot, that gave performances every day. And more easily than in Constantinople, I found Oriental music and dancing, in certain Halsted Street cafés.

Here you may order a cup of Turkish coffee, aromatic and velvety, and a narghile of Persian tobacco, and watch an elaborate shadow play in colors, depicting the adventures of a traditional comic character, a form of entertainment which even in Stamboul is being superseded by the movie. Or, as you listen to the merry bubbling of your water pipe, you may see the young men dancing in a ring, as they dance on feast days in some village square in the mountains of Macedonia. Or you may watch a young girl in an ancient dance of the East, that is half gypsy. Standing with her head in her hands, drooping first to one side, then to another, with a look of agony on her features, her voice rises in a plaintive wail, shaken as though by sobs. Then, as the music suddenly changes to a mad rhythm, frantically gay, she begins to dance, her arms and body swaying in swift, voluptuous movements. The dancing is often followed by the singing of old ballads commemorating the countless border frays in the history of the Near East.

Interesting and picturesque as are the various races to be seen on Halsted, none are as exotic and colorful as the gypsies, although they seem out of place on city streets. As I passed the Maxwell Street market, amid the cries of Jewish venders and the clucking, quacking, and honking of poultry in piles of crates, I caught sight of a cage of Canada geese—graceful birds with trim black plumage, the shyest and shrewdest of game, the heralds of spring. Like the gypsies, they seemed lost in the noisy, stifling slum.

Continuing on Halsted to Monroe, I found a crowd of Nomads drinking Budweiser from bottles in the "Workingmen's Exchange." It is one of the little ironies of nomenclature that of two saloons in Chicago which bore this name, one was Hinky Dink's, the favorite hang-out of the hobo, and the other this rendezvous of idle gypsies. One or two were old acquaintances, who called to me in joyous greeting, *"Sar mai san, Kolya?"* and invited me to join the long line at the bar. One of the women came in to get a sandwich at the free-lunch counter without even spending a nickel for beer, whereupon one of the men cried to her, *"Počines te piav?"* ("Will you pay for the drinks?") to which she assented. *"Kuč sandwiča"* ("Expensive sandwich"), remarked my neighbor as she handed the barkeeper several dollars.

To pay was considered an honor, and most of
[145]

the gypsies were wealthy. One of them, who was a bit tipsy, drew from his pocket at intervals a roll of bills containing six thousand dollars. He was having an argument with another *Rom,* and from time to time they would almost come to blows. The next moment they would throw their arms about each other and kiss on the cheeks.

Toasts resounded on all sides, for Romanies never tire of drinking one another's health. Crossing the necks of bottles and clinking them first on one side and then on the other, they wished one another health, wealth, and luck in an endless variety of ways: *"T'aves baXtalo! But sastimus! Sastipe! But love! But čave! Del o Del BaXt! Nais tuke, prala!"* In expressions of this sort it is the world's richest language.

There was a piano in the room, and one of the gypsies, Serga, who had been on the stage, began to play, while the others sang in chorus. Their deep bass voices were rich and full; and it was not long before a crowd of children's heads completely filled the space beneath the swinging doors of the saloon. Singing, however, was against either a city ordinance or the rules of the saloon, and the proprietor and bartender did their best to stop it. "All right, boss, we'll stop," the gypsies replied, politely, and went on singing, even after the piano had been shut and locked.

Having had sufficient to drink and not wishing

to insult my hosts by refusing, I went for a walk. When I returned that night about ten o'clock there was only one Romani left at the bar, the famous "king of the gypsies," Joe Adams, or Ioano, as he was known to his own people. Ioano, alas! was a king in exile, a dethroned potentate; but he carried himself with regal bearing. He was tall and strong, and in looks, at least, he was every inch a king.

Some ten years before he had been the acknowledged leader of a large tribe; but another gypsy chief, Zlačo Dimitrio, had evolved a plan whereby the various clans of Nomads should be united under a single ruler, himself. A large meeting was held near Chicago, which was attended by several hundred families. Each family was to pay the chief a fixed annual tax, in return for which they were to receive protection in case they got into trouble with the police. To defend them the best lawyers were to be hired with funds from the royal treasury.

Fearing that this was simply a scheme to fill Zlačo's pocket, Ioano protested, and endeavored to form a rival organization. He claimed that Zlačo had defrauded his brother of seventy gold napoleons, and took the matter into court. It was a great mistake and he forfeited the sympathy of the Romanies. As Zlačo had larger funds behind him, he won. In chagrin Ioano began to drink. "Our leader is mad," said the tribesmen who had remained faithful to him, and, meeting in council, they finally deposed him.

Ioano was born in Austria. Early in life he had won his roving chiefdom by his strength of arm, his courage, and sheer dominance. Marriages with his relatives were as much sought after as in any court of Europe; and numerous families were added to his tribe in this manner. Others simply placed themselves beneath his protection. Wherever he chose to go they followed; and his wanderings took them far and wide on the face of the globe.

It was closing time before I knew it; and even kings must obey barkeeps. At the cry of, "One o'clock! Everybody out!" we were forced to leave, much to Ioano's annoyance. Remembering my reserve fund, I took a room for the night in a hotel over a saloon on Madison Street, and had a case of beer sent up to us. It is not every day that one has the privilege of entertaining royalty.

It was seven o'clock when the last bottle was emptied. "There is a trial this morning. I must go to it. Will you come?" Completely at his command, I followed him first to a bar, where he tossed off three fingers of Greek brandy by way of breakfast, next to a pawnshop, where he pledged a large gold coin bearing the image of Louis IV, and finally to the Stock-yards Police Court, where the trial was in progress. It was the case of the wife, Jiva, who had left her husband and had been accused of taking his money with her, described in the chapter, "Love Among the Gypsies."

Not only was the court room overflowing, but also the neighboring saloons—and saloons were not lacking. At one time there was a solid half a mile of them in a single street in the stock-yards district. Being disgusted with the progress of the trial—or thirsty—Ioano slipped out. I found him later in a bar, having a heated argument in regard to the trial. His opponent was Dusan, a relative of the man who had been abandoned. The fact that Dusan had been an ardent supporter of Zlačo Dimitrio, and that the woman's family had remained loyal to Ioano, added fuel to the flame. Dusan taunted the former chief with having lost his authority and with being a drunkard. "You are drunk now" *("San mato akano")*.

Ioano's eyes flashed with anger, but he kept his kingly dignity. "Dusan," he said, *"či k'erdiom mišto,* I did not do right when I had Zlačo arrested, ten years ago. But our people were blinded by him. Would they have given my brother justice? Your family did wrong in having Jiva arrested now. Why should the *Gaje* know of our affairs? And as for being drunk, we shall see; we shall have an ordeal. Will you drink with me, glass for glass?" Dusan accepted, and the strange fight began. Whisky after

[149]

whisky had been swallowed by each of the contestants, when I returned to the court to watch the progress of the trial.

The case having been dismissed, I returned to the bar to see the outcome of the whisky duel. On reaching the swinging doors I heard a buzz of excited voices and the shrill cry of a woman. A crowd of gypsies was surging about a table on which Dusan lay stretched at full length, unconscious. He was lifted and carried to a taxi-cab, to be taken to his camp on the edge of the city. Standing at the bar, watching the proceedings impassively, was Ioano, as calm and majestic as ever. "Come, let us go, brother," was his only remark.

It was five o'clock. Not having closed my eyes for thirty-six hours, I wanted to sleep. Ioano offered a bed in his own establishment, but suggested that, as there were a dozen small grandchildren constantly running about and shouting, I would get very little sleep. I obtained a room in a cheap hotel on Halsted. As soon as I had closed the door, Ioano turned to me and asked, "How much money have you?" I was not in any position to make a loan, but his tone was firm, and I told him. "Give it to me!" he commanded. Was he begging, borrowing, or holding me up, I wondered? His voice and manner were so imperious that I gave it to him—to the last cent. When he had gone I lay down, but remained

[150]

An argument

awake for some time, puzzling over the situation.

When I awoke it was dark. I had not the faintest idea of the hour. Leaving the hotel to stroll down Halsted, I found it was about eleven. A block away I looked in the open door of a saloon usually frequented by hobos because of the huge size of the beers, and there was Ioano standing at the bar in front of an empty glass. *"Haide,"* he said, *"kamav te piav woreso"* ("Come, I want to drink something"), as though he had not been drinking steadily for two days and nights. He led the way to the hotel bar and ordered two glasses of beer. I would much rather have had my money, but I waited for a good opportunity to ask for it. When he had finished, the bartender said, with a snarl, "Well, what the —— yuh waitin' for?"

"I haven't any money. You pay him," said Ioano, nonchalantly, to me.

"But I gave you all I had," I replied, my heart sinking at the prospect of being stone broke in Chicago. By this time the bartender was cursing us both with every oath he could think of, but Ioano eyed him as indifferently as an elephant might eye a mosquito.

"That is true. Wait here," answered Ioano. A moment later he returned and handed me an envelope. On it was scrawled, "Joe, King of the Gypsies." It contained my money. "I took it so no one would steal it," he explained. "When my own money was gone I was afraid I might spend yours; so I gave it to the clerk to keep. You see I was very thirsty."

We went to the "Workingmen's Exchange," to make a last effort toward quenching his thirst, but the task was hopeless. He drank to forget the indignity of having been dethroned by his subjects; but drink as he might, he could not even attain the longed-for oblivion. Only death could bring that. Well, to drink himself to death was as good a way as another. A man at the piano was singing "Tipperary." Misunderstanding the words, Ioano joined in the chorus in his broken English:

> " 'It's a longk way to dee cemetery,
> It's a longk ways to go . . .' "

It was what was uppermost in his thoughts.

There is no race of people that loves life as much as the gypsies, as Borrow has pointed out in one of the most poetic pages in English prose. When one of them has ceased to care for night and day, for sun, moon, and stars, and the wind on the heath, you may be sure that his cup of bitterness is full indeed.

The path to the cemetery, which had seemed so long, proved shorter than he had hoped. Not long after, the news spread throughout the tribes, "Ioano is dead."

From time to time the few who remained faith-

ful return to hold a funeral feast and pour libations on his grave, according to their custom; but
although they mourn his loss most bitterly, they
know it is well that his aching heart has ceased
to throb, and his proud spirit, that found the
wide world a narrow cage, is free at last.

CHAPTER VI

SOME ANGLO-AMERICAN ROMANIES

THERE is no branch of the Romani race as much beloved as those from England. They are the least wild and shy; but much of their charm comes from the contrast of their apparent tameness with their roguishness and the mystery of their hidden ways. Even among the well-to-do house dwellers of mixed stock in this country one finds many genuine gypsy traits and survivals of ancient customs brought from India.

The automobile, which has helped to keep the Nomads ever wandering, has caused the *Romaničels,* as the English gypsies here call themselves, to settle down. The latter were almost exclusively horse dealers, making large profits on arriving in this country. Many of them bought land, which was then very cheap. They did not settle on it, however, to any great extent until the commonness of the gasoline engine made horse dealing unprofitable. Now the majority live on farms and in towns, at least during the cold months. In many cases the land they bought on the outskirts of various cities years ago is to-day in the heart of business sections, and is worth hundreds of thousands of dollars.

Some found themselves thus enriched, but nearly all lost their rights to the property by failure to pay the taxes. Frequently they left their land, and thought no more about it. "My granddad owned Hoboken Hill," said one of the Boswells, "but we moved West, and traveled there for fifty years. We'd all be millionaires now if he'd kep' it. Well, what's the difference! I didn't have no *wongur,* no money, when I comed into this here world, and the dear Lord 'll not let me take it with me when I goes.

"Money ain't everythink. It ain't so much what you *got* as how you feels about it. Take old-man Sampson and his *jivel* [his wife], Delighty. They'se got a big ranch near Indianapolis what they rents fer enough to live like kings; but they lives around where anyone 'll let 'em *tan* [camp]. Each does their own cookin'; and they never speaks one to the other. Money never done them no good, now, did it, young mon?"

I was forced to agree; but I wanted to add that a couple named Sampson and Delighty, the latter name being a corruption of Delilah, could hardly be expected to live in harmony.

During the winter following my first meeting with gypsies in Spain I had studied all the

Romani words in the writings of Borrow and Leland, and had chanced on Smart & Crofton's *Dialect of the English Gypsies,* which gave me my first insight into gypsy grammar.

Spring came. The wild ducks had flown northward. Each time I had watched the V-shaped lines dwindle into the distance my heartstrings would tighten and the longing for gypsies would increase. The majority of Romanies spend the winter in the Southern States like the migratory birds, appearing in Wisconsin only as the weather grows mild. Many an afternoon I spent in vain search, until one Saturday late in May.

I had started eastward from Madison along the old Willow Walk beside the Lake, past the ruined mill and the dam with its curtain of white water, now a dignified lock, and out into the country, circling about through country lanes and across fields. It was a beautiful walk—but no gypsies. I passed a hillside white with apple trees in bloom. The warm breeze shook the branches and showers of petals drifted on the air like butterflies. They fell to rest and I resumed my search somewhat sadly. Coming into Lover's Lane, I found the smooth lilac bushes touched with lavender. There was a faint suggestion of perfume in the air.

There at the end of the lane, in a pasture opposite the Corners, I saw the tents and the wagons. In one of the saloons at the crossroads

A camp of the Wells family in New Jersey.
Many Romaničels *still use horses and wagons*

I found a gypsy, a man about thirty-five years of age, who was standing in the center of a group of farmers, loafers, and Romanies. He was Nick Yerne, a Romani of mixed blood, but nevertheless a typical gypsy, save in physical strength. One of his arms was slightly crippled by an accident; but the weakness of this limb was amply compensated by the sharpness of his wits and by the cheerfulness of his disposition. According to his mother, he had fits of black despondency, but, like a true aristocrat, he hid them even from his friends. He was always making others laugh.

Nick was slight of build, with aquiline features, curly chestnut hair, and smiling lips. His brown eyes were always dancing with delight, and at the same time they were taking in everything about him. His glance was as merry and as penetrating as a ray of sunlight. As for his temperament, he was as reckless as he was shrewd.

His mother, Sybil, was a Yerne, which is a corruption of Herne or Heron, one of the truest families of English gypsies. She was a famous fortune teller, and from her he had gained his keen insight into human nature and his joyousness. Like many gypsies, he used his mother's family name. His father, strange to say, was a Quaker. From him he seemed to have inherited no traits, unless a certain canny shrewdness is a Quaker characteristic.

He traded more than all the other gypsies in

the camp together, for not only was he a better judge of horses, but also a better judge of men. He had no more compunction about cheating a *Gajo* than the rest; but he felt that honesty—or better still, a reputation for honesty—was the best policy, and his judgment was justified by the host of farmers and dealers through the Middle West who were eager to trade with him.

He knew every trick by which a true horse may be made to seem worthless and a "killer" may be made to seem sound; but he had graduated beyond that stage. This knowledge, however, kept him from being imposed on. In his apprentice days he had practiced such tricks as taking a horse that was lame in one leg and blistering the other temporarily so that its gait would be even, and of administering judicial doses of strychine or heroin to give life to a worn-out plug, for the time being, or of rubbing tallow on the teeth of a healthy animal, while examining it, in order to make it refuse to eat, so that the owner would be glad to get rid of it cheap, and of rubbing a gentle horse with Spanish fly to make it balk. But he only used these trickeries on special occasions, and gave his attention to the owner rather than to the horse.

There was no one like Nick to convince a man that his horse needed a good trading. By the time Nick had finished talking to him he was hypnotized into believing that the gypsy was doing him a favor by taking it off his hands.

On the rare occasions when he traded a "killer," he took the crowd into his confidence and made a joke of it, so that everyone would be certain that he was open and aboveboard. His chief asset was his sense of comedy. He was a born actor, like all gypsies; and the moment people knew that he was in town they would come to trade with him in order to have a good laugh— even at their own expense.

The afternoon I first met him a characteristic incident occurred. A Norwegian farmer was boasting of his knowledge of horseflesh and the fine mare he had bought that morning. He was so happy at having had the best of the bargain that he had celebrated by consuming an undue quantity of acquavit at Ole Moens', and had stopped for one more drink, at the Corners, the last chance. Nick led him on until his bragging about having cheated the other fellow made the crowd disgusted. The Romani's next move was to play on the farmer's pride until he was eager to give an exhibition of his skill at trading.

At the proper moment Nick spoke to one of the gypsy boys who was standing near, *"Ja anar the gruvni akai!"* I was puzzled by what he said, for, instead of bringing a cow as he was directed, the boy brought a spirited black horse. "No, not that one!" said Nick, loudly, adding in gypsy, *"Ava, adova si"* ("Yes, that's it"). Then, as though he were still talking to the boy, he continued: "What did you bring that one for? That's a pleasure horse. The gentleman 'ere wants a plow 'orse what he can 'itch to his buggy when he takes his wife to town." As the farmer was noted for being wealthy but very close-fisted, the crowd was amused.

"No," said the Norwegian, somewhat nettled, "Ei tink dat yüst süit me." After wrangling for twenty minutes Nick consented to give him the black in exchange for the mare he had purchased that morning and ten dollars to boot if he would stand treat.

"Well," said Nick when the bargain was concluded, "ain't you goin' to treat the crowd?" The farmer had hoped to get away without even buying Nick a drink, and it was with great reluctance that he bought one for all, especially as Nick got the thanks.

When he had gone, the gypsy put them all in a good humor, treating liberally, cracking jokes, and intimating that he had just played a trick for their amusement. One would have thought Nick's sole joy in life was to entertain the dealers, farmers, and loafers that swarmed about the bar. Desirous of winning the gypsy's favor myself, I offered to follow his example by paying for a round of drinks. Quickly, and almost angrily, he checked me, saying, *"Kek!* They're *Gajos!"*

("Don't! They're Gentiles!") The scorn with which he said *"Gajos"* showed that he was merely playing a farce.

"Here he comes back!" shouted some one who was standing at the door. We all flocked to see, and there, driving up the road, was the farmer in a towering rage. From quite a distance every breath of the horse sounded like the roaring of a forge. It had the heaves. No wonder Nick had called it a *gruvni,* a cow, for at every step it seemed to be mooing. The farmer's features, already red from drinking, blazed a deep crimson with wrath and humiliation. "Stand by me, boys!" said Nick in a tone that expected no wavering. Immediately I understood why he had been at such pains to humor the hangers-on in the saloon. Like the farmer, they were mostly Norwegians; but instead of siding with their fellow countryman they were with Nick to a man. Although the fellow was over six feet tall and could have felled the gypsy with one blow, a solid wall of brawn barred the way.

On another occasion, about a year later, I saw Nick trade a kicker to a Jewish spectacle peddler. The man made a living selling glasses to country people who were too ignorant to consult an oculist. Those whose eyes were good were almost certain to have them ruined if they bought from him; and those whose eyes were bad were sure to have them made worse. Knowing that no one would have the slightest sympathy for the fellow if he were worsted in a deal, Nick laid his plans.

It was dusk when the peddler stopped at the saloon on his way to the city. Nick and Chisindine Lee, another Romani, were playing cards. Seeing that the man had a good horse, Nick spoke in gypsy to Chisy's boy, Isaiah, and told him to bring two horses and tether them near the tents. One was a horse with glanders, and the other, a bay mare, was the kicker. Without interrupting his game of pitch, Nick glanced through the barroom door, praised the Jew's horse, and suggested a trade. At the word trade the peddler was immediately interested. "How much you give me?"

Nick examined the animal thoroughly, praised the good points that were most obvious, pretended to overlook certain minor blemishes, and offered slightly more than it was worth. "Haha! a greenhorn!" the fellow must have thought; and he demanded a larger amount.

"That's more 'n I got," said Nick, "but I'll trade you." He was well aware that the man would rather make an exchange, as he would have to have a horse to pull his buggy. Walking over to the tents, Nick offered the one with the glanders, but the man refused to consider it.

"How about the other one?" he said, pointing to the kicker, a bay mare that was young and sound, a splendid-looking animal.

"No," replied Nick, "I can't trade you that." But as the peddler insisted, he agreed to do so for a good sum in addition. At that moment Mrs. Lee, who had been given her cue in gypsy, came out of the tent and, pretending to be Nick's wife, pleaded with him not to sell: "Don't let Sally go! We raised her from a colt. And she's so spry and gentle." When Nick insisted that they needed the money for a doctor for the baby, Mrs. Lee came near him and whispered just loud enough for the man to hear: "Get him to take one of the others. Sally's the only sound horse you've got." Nick agreed to keep the mare, and, as the Jew would not take the glandered horse, the gypsies retired to the saloon and resumed their game of cards. But the peddler had swallowed the bait, hook and all. From an offer to trade for the good-looking kicker, he gradually increased the amount he was willing to pay in addition, while Nick and Chisy, apparently absorbed in their game of pitch, pretended not to be interested. From time to time the gypsy would offer to show him other horses in the morning, but as for the bay mare, he had decided not to sell it, anyway. Besides, it was getting late and he did not feel like trading. The more reluctance he seemed to show, the more eager the peddler was to make the deal; and finally, after a handsome offer, Nick accepted. He pocketed the money and hitched up the bay for the peddler.

Half an hour later the expected happened. Hearing the hoofbeats down the road, he recognized them, though he had had the mare only a day. Hurrying to where the peddler's horse was tethered, he hid it, while the rest of us retired to the darkened tents. Willing to sacrifice the money if he could get his own horse back again, the man made a search for it, and finally found it. As he was leading it to his buggy, the dashboard of which had been kicked to pieces, the gypsies pounced on him.

"What are you doing with my horse?" yelled Nick.

"You cheat me. I want my horse back." He was almost weeping with fear and rage. "Take that she-devil, and give me my horse back!"

Although they were ready to burst with laughter, the gypsies pretended to be angry. "I didn't want to trade, nohow, but I had to do something to get rid of you. I'm sick of tradin' with a man as don't *depreciate* a nice lively animal. But maybe Mr. Lee here can fix you up." The peddler was willing to take anything rather than drive the kicker again; and it was easy for Chisy to pass off an old horse that he had been trying to get rid of for some time.

Each month a horse market was held in Madison; and each month in summer I would go to various camping places in hopes of finding Nick. How I looked forward to his visits! Spying me from afar as I approached the tent, he would let out a war whoop like a wild Indian. He was always glad to see me, since he could be himself. With my firm conviction, at the time, that I could boast of gypsy ancestry, it was not surprising that he, too, was convinced of it, and would confide to me that he got so sick of *Gajos* that he would drive out of his way for days just to see a Romani face and speak the beloved tongue, *raker* a *bita Romanes*.

If his regard for the Gentiles was a fine bit of acting, they never knew it; and there was not a single man that frequented the crossroads who did not miss him from the moment his wagon pulled out of the pasture until it returned. If a farmer had a plow to be loaded on his wagon, it was Nick who would cry: "Come on, boys! Let's give him a hand!" And although he lifted the least, he would grunt the loudest and make a joke of the heaviest task.

There was a charming old drunkard who acted as porter in the saloon, and who lived on memories of the days when he had been the coachman of a Governor of Wisconsin. He also lived on anticipation of Nick's visits, for the liquor would be sure to flow with the utmost freedom.

If the gypsy had a sense of humor, he also had abandon. One Fourth of July he laid a bet that his horse could beat Orny Young's in a half-mile race to a certain bridge over a swampy creek, the loser to jump into the water, clothes and all. He lost. If Orny had not been a *Romaničel,* Nick would have found a satisfactory excuse for not keeping the agreement, but his word to another gypsy was final. Handing me the reins, he stood up in the buggy and dove head foremost over the bridge rail into the shallow water and oozy mud. It was a moment before he could extricate himself; but he emerged, covered with black slime, the first to laugh at his plight.

Each month, a few days before the horse market, there were sure to be gypsies camped near Lovers' Lane or beside the thicket near Lake Wingra. One week, never to be forgotten, there appeared four of the tribes of truest blood, the aristocracy of Gypsydom, the Lockes, the Smiths, the Boswells, and the Lovells.

There was Aunt Eppy Locke, still beautiful despite her twoscore years, with snaky black curls, and eyes that danced and sparkled like jet and seemed to go right through you. How often, in her younger days, that glance must have set the blood leaping in the veins of *Romaničels* and *Gajos!* And how often that ready laughter must have kept the lightning from striking, and that soft smile have been a healing balm to shattered hearts.

There was kindly Asa Smith, whom I thought

I had offended by not accepting his urgent invitation to share his four-o'clock meal of broiled mutton and huckleberries, but who set me at ease when he found me supping a little later with Julia and Clarence Smith, saying: "That's all right, young mon. He's my son." Accepting hospitality from a member of the family pleased him as much as though I had accepted it from him.

There was Davy Boswell, whose skin was the color of old mahogany. No *Gajo* blood in Davy. He was extremely active; and when not trading horses he was always making baskets, which he wove with the utmost deftness. He spoke seldom; but when he did his grown sons jumped to obey.

It was a relative of Davy's, I believe, who had two wives, a proceeding sanctioned by gypsy custom, but rare. As *Romaničel* women are often the chief breadwinners, and frequently carry the bank roll, they are inclined to giving orders; and what man wants to be ruled by two women?

It was a treat to have found these "real old-fashioned *Romaničels*" so early in my gypsying. The Boswell-Lovell tribe was from Wales and the English border region; and was probably the one described by Watts-Dunton in his novel *Alwyn,* which contains the immortal Sinfie Lovell, drawn from life.

In those days I was thrilled by the mere mention of *patterans,* or *patrins,* the secret marks by which the Romani trail is indicated to those who follow. And sure enough, the afternoon I met them a handsome young couple drove up at dusk and the man called out, "Who turned the *patrin?*" They had found the branch which was to mark the way at a crossroads pointing in the wrong direction, making them lose an hour or two in search of the camp. "It must have been some of them bloody Turks," Webster answered, blaming everything on the Nomads, as is the custom with the *Romaničels.*

As the peace of night settled down on the camp, we gathered in a circle about an open fire to spend an hour or two in chat. Conversation to the Romani is both bridge and books. Each had a story to tell, and all were ready listeners.

Fontella Lovell related how an aunt of hers had fallen in love with a preacher man in the *puro tem* (the old country) ; and in spite of her father's threats to kill her if she married a *Gajo,* and in spite of the determination of the *rašai's* congregation to have him expelled from church if he took a heathen to wed, they had run off together, the preacher himself performing his own ceremony when the one in the next town had turned them away.

"Well," concluded Fontella, "it was good in the sight of my dearie *Duvel* [the Lord], as my dear aunt used to say. They were happy 'til he died, though he didn't like to have her *dŭkker,* and the life on the roads was hard on him, he was so soft. But he'd say, 'As long as you don't try to fool anyone, as long as you believe what you say, you can tell fortunes.' The *rašais* is only *dŭkkermengros,* after all; and there's many a man in the Holy Book that used to go around fortellin' the future. He'd say, too, 'Maybe us *Gajos* has lived so long in four walls that we've shut out the sound of God's voice, so long under roofs that we can't read the signs in the sky.' But when she saw the rough life was killing him, she'd beg him to settle down, though a house would 'a' choked her; but he'd say, 'Didn't the Lord tell his followers to go their way without purse or shoes, to bless them as gave, and never think about food nor dress, for seein' my dearie *Duvel* feeds the birds and clothes the good green earth with grass and flowers.' But I'm thinkin' they'd 'a' died more 'n once if she hadn't *čord* a chicken now and then and told him the farmers had give' it to her."

Other tales were of humor or heroism. Uncle Davy told how, in the days when he "didn't care for hell nor high water," he had knocked out with one punch a murderer, the terror of the West Virginia mountains. Asa related how he and his family had nearly been lynched once in a Missouri village when his horse fell in the street and the crowd gathering about had heard his parrot inside the wagon crying: "Dear! Oh dear! Let me out!" Of course they thought it was a kidnapped child, and were about to hang him to a telegraph pole as quickly as possible and investigate afterward, when the arrival of the sheriff made them change their plans.

As the conversation shifted back to the subject of *Gajos* being attracted by Romanies, another of the Smiths narrated his experiences with a Gentile widow who fell in love with him when camping near East St. Louis. As he rode by her house she called to him from her window and begged him to stop. *Paš mulo* (half dead) from a long day in the saddle, he consented. For his entertainment she sent for a bottle of rum and a couple of colored girls to play the banjo and sing for him. "She was a proper lady, and kept a tellin' the *kaler raklis* [the girls] not to spit their tobacco juice on the parlor floor. And a *rinkni pivli* [a pretty widow] she was, with hair that hung to her feet." She told him how she had stood at the window for hours waiting for him to pass, and now when he got up to leave she had thrown her arms about him and begged him to take her with him to travel the roads.

Vilolia Lovell commented: "She'd 'a' left you quick enough. *Gajos* and *Romaničels* can't never mix."

"How about the preacher?" I asked.

"Well, he was a simple man and a good one. There *is* good *Gajos,* you know, though I never seen one. But do you think if he'd 'a' knowed that the chickens he ate was coaxed into his wife's sack when nobody was lookin', and that she *dŭkkered* in *lubnitans,* and drank her beer, her *kusi levinor,* and joked with the men in pubs, do you think he'd 'a' understood? No, he wouldn't, though I've heard him talk about Mary Magdalene bein' a *lubni* and a friend of Christ, and our dear Lord 'sociatin' with public-house keepers. No, *Gajos* don't understand nothingk."

In proof of her statement she cited a recent occurence at a county fair. A rural Don Juan, misinterpreting her frank gaze and smiles as admiration, had passed from coarse jollying to improper proposals. Vilolia had said nothing until she had finished the "reading" and obtained all the money she could. Then she spoke her mind. As he slunk away she followed him through the crowd, giving him a tongue lashing as only a gypsy can, and repeating all his remarks in loud, angry tones, while the farmers' wives eyed him indignantly and the men snickered. "I follied him fer a block, the *jukel,"* she said. "And him with his eyes on the ground, like he was lookin' fer a leaf to crawl under and hide."

As the fire died down and the circle of light grew smaller and smaller, the gypsies gradually retired to their tents, and as I walked home under the elms, whose branches bent as though in kindly blessing, I thought of the Welsh preacher who had found true love among the gypsies, and true religion by the wayside. He had found life because he had not been afraid of casting it away. He had lived, while those who had turned him from their churches had vegetated in their villages, forgetful of the words, "Woe unto you, scribes and Pharisees, hypocrites! for ye are as graves which appear not, and the men that walk over them are not aware of them."

Of the various Romanies who have forsaken the tent and the van for positions of distinction in *Gajo* society none is better known or better loved than Rodney Smith, the gypsy evangelist. In view of the fact that the gypsies are anything but a religious race, it seems surprising; but they are an artistic race, and the line between art and religion is as invisible as a line of latitude— except on paper.

His father was a fiddler, fond of the flowing bowl. In the taverns where he played, Rodney would dance and pass the hat. At other times he peddled clothes pegs that were whittled in camp; and his wit, his whimsical sayings, and his gift of softening hearts found ready buyers, just as in later days they were to find eager listeners to his preaching.

The beginning of his conversion was *Pilgrim's*

Progress, read by a young man in a public house. As Bunyan was probably a gypsy, or at least a tinker, it seems quite natural that his influence on a Romani should have been so deep. Rodney walked to the house where Bunyan had lived, and, standing there, he wept and longed to find the same Jesus Christ that had made the author of *Pilgrim's Progress* what he was.

Determined to learn how to read, Gypsy Smith, then an adolescent, found a primer in the huge letters of a brewery sign. From then on he gradually rose to his present pre-eminence in his calling.

During the war I heard him speak in a large tent in New York, fascinating his audience by the very traits that seem most gypsy. There was no false humility, no hypocrisy, no fanaticism. He was natural, human, magnetic with the heart-felt eloquence of the poet rather than the orator. And although his images had an Oriental exuberance, they glowed with emotion, and their exuberance was that of nature. "I have seen God take the colors from the flowers," he said, "and, making a scarf, He wrapped it around the shoulders of the storm—a rainbow." On another's lips the phrase might have been mere bombast. Other images were no less effective: "A time will come when the stars will go out, like the sparks from a blacksmith's forge."

In addition to his magnetism and native gift

for self-expression, which few gypsies lack, he had a mellow sense of humor, and he showed, when later he led the singing, a genuine feeling for music. But what impressed me most was the warm friendliness that radiated from the man, the love which most gypsies reserve for their fellow Romani alone. When the meeting was over, hundreds of people pressed about him to touch his hand, with an eagerness that I have seen on only one other occasion—when the crowd swarmed into a Spanish bull ring to acclaim a gypsy torero, El Gitanillo de Riclas. When I was able to approach the evangelist I spoke to him in *Romanes,* and saw by the light in his eyes that, although he loved the whole world, his love for his own race burned deepest in his heart.

I have seen the same phenomenon in other Romanies who have become "civilized." Once in Washington, D. C., some tent dwellers took me to the apartment of another family of gypsies. There were books, a grand piano, and an excellent reproduction of Whistler's portrait of his mother; but prosperity and culture had not made them lose their simple hospitality and kindliness toward those of the same blood.

If there are many gypsies who live like *Gajos,* there are also many *Gajos* who live like gypsies. Every horse trader who lives in tent and wagon is not necessarily a gypsy. In addition to native Americans who have adopted this mode of life,

[174]

I have met in this country the so-called English "travelers," the Irish "travelers," and the Scotch "gypsies." The Irish "travelers," or tinkers, are an amusing lot, of which the well-known Jennings tribe is a typical example. They only lack a Synge to chronicle their exploits. Some of them speak a little *Romanes* in addition to English, but their secret language is either modern cant or Shelta, a tongue discovered by Leland, which is an old Irish Gælic back-slang or rhyming cant, extremely ancient.

A characteristic Scotch gypsy was my friend Jim Stuart, who, after traveling for years in Galloway, traveled the Middle West in a covered wagon that was the exact image of a prairie schooner. Though Scoto-Romani is a decidedly broken language, Jim's *Romanes* was fairly good; and I learned from him a number of words that are common only in the purer dialects. As his light hair and ruddy features were anything but Romani, I was mystified, until in a recent number of the *Journal* of the Gypsy Lore Society I read of a member of the aristocratic Scotch family of Stuarts who many generations ago had joined the gypsies. Jim was doubtless a descendant, and prided himself on being a gypsy, as his ancestors had prided themselves on being related to kings, though he must have had as much royal blood as Romani.

Over a glass of beer in a country saloon one

day, he told me that the week before, as he was
leaving his camp, he had met a farmer coming
down the road with a shotgun, swearing to chase
"them —— —— gypsies outa there!" Being a
splendid-looking Scotch type and neatly dressed,
the farmer did not dream of associating Jim with
the covered wagon. With a smile my friend
remarked unconcernedly to the wrathful fellow:
"I just passed there and had a good look at them.
They ain't gypsies at all." Appeased, the farmer
shouldered his gun and walked back to the house.
"And me as good a Romani as the best!" he
added, with a grin of delight.

Jim was one of the few really happy men I
have ever known, and was almost as popular with
Gajos and gypsies as Nick Yerne. He had a
veritable passion for seeing people happy; and,
although relatively abstemious himself, his generosity in providing others with joyous drink or
entertainment was princely. Swinging his boy
to the top of the table, he asked him to give us a
song and dance. The little lad was as much delighted as the onlookers. But if only the stately
ancestor might have seen this noble scion of the
Stuarts!

Only once did Jim ever confess to having been
unhappy. "Last year I wintered in Chicago,
and it seemed like spring 'u'd never come. Some
days I'd go out and sit in the stable with the
horses, just so it 'u'd seem like I was on the road

again." He had felt the undying wanderlust that had made his ancestor put into practice the words of the old song:

"I'm off with the raggle-taggle gypsies O!"

I have met a number of families of *poš-rats,* or half-bloods, many of whom had only a slight admixture of Romani blood in their veins. The pure *Romaničels* are clean, courteous, and loyal to their kind; but the *poš-rats* are a mixed lot in more senses than one. The true gypsies often warned me against certain families: "Look out for the Traceys! They're a bad lot!" or, "Keep clear of the fightin' Harrisons!" Had I met them I might have found them friendly enough; though it is these half-and-halfs that have given the gypsy race a bad name.

Once in the Northeast I found a certain family that I had been warned against. They had settled down and had sent their sons to a veterinary school to learn all the tricks of doping horses. One of the boys had even extracted information from a professor in an agricultural college; but it only proved to be a stepping-stone to the penitentiary. "It's a rotten town," the mother confided to me. "They'll *lel* you *opré* for *čiči* [arrest you for nothing at all]. It's ag'in' the law to dope horses [*bik driz*], do any bootleggin', or *sima covas* as was *čored* [to pawn

[177]

stolen goods]. In fact, it's gettin' so you can't make an honest livin'."

They were cordial, but how different from pure-blooded Romanies like Johnston Boswell— God love him! When I knew him he was over seventy and lived in a little hut of his own building on the outskirts of a Canadian city. Most of his life had been spent on the road in England and North America. His father lived to be one hundred and two, and his grandfather one hundred and three. "When us *Romaničels* lives indoors we dies off quick—like the Indians." But although he had slept under a roof for some time, he was as active as a boy.

It was a crisp April day when I first met him. The sun was bright and the smooth gray trunks and velvety buds of the maple trees were oozing sap. He was sitting at the door of his hut, silently absorbing the beauty of the spring. "When the days are shiny, us *Romaničels* can't stay inside. Everything is wakin' up, same as they'd been asleep. Plants have feelin's. *Dawdi, dawdi!* I'd just like to dive head first into that pile of straw!"

The only sign of advancing age one could discover in Johnston was his tendency to lament the "good old times." "Nowadays us gypsies is gettin' too edicated. Some of my nephews is bein' raised as lawyers and they ain't half so smart as them as couldn't read nor write. An-

other teaches arthurletics in a school, but he ain't
half so strong nor so quick as his dear cousin
what can carry a pony on his back and can jump
a six-foot fence. The race is run out. The
Gajos is learnin' *Romanes,* and we's learnin'
Gajo ways. There was a time when a *Romaničel* would take off his boots and pawn 'em to help
you. Now he'd put on his cast-iron shoes and
kick you clean to hell." The last remark was a
libel, as Boswell's hospitable example proved;
but I was forced to agree with the next one.
"Canady and America's gettin' worse than the
puro tem. You got to get permission for every-
thingk. It's gettin' too automatic." He meant
autocratic, but he was not far wrong.

It was a pleasure to hear him tell about his
father, who was six feet one, with a silky beard,
always well combed, and was "the best fiddler in
Canady." He loved the beautiful old songs that
had been handed down in his family for centuries,
and that no one else knew. "In the pubs and
saloons they was always beggin' him to play
somethink from the music 'alls, or somethink they
could dance to; but if he didn't feel like it, he
wouldn't play, not for *oanč bar* [five pounds].
It was only the swells what 'preciated his playin';
and they'd come for miles to hear him."

Boswell had a theory of the origin of the
gypsies that was certainly ingenious. He had
seen them dwelling in tents in England, and

wandering from place to place, much like the copper-skinned aborigines of America. "Us Romanies is the Indians of England."

It happened that one day the fact that the gypsies are East Indians was well demonstrated before Johnston's very eyes. A British ex-soldier who had served in India used to drop in occasionally to talk about England. One day when the former Tommy told me that he spoke Hindustani, I asked him the name for a number of objects which were practically the same in *Romanes*. As he gave them I saw a look of astonishment spread over Johnston's face. With his eyes fairly popping as he heard the Hindustani, he exclaimed, "Why, that's *poš-Romanes!* It's broken gypsy!"

Johnston never spoke the *kalo jib* before *Gajos*. His father had taught that it was a deadly sin, "ag'in' the gypsy religion," to do so; and the brother of a famous singer who had lived with them for a summer had managed to pick up but a single word—*rakli*—the word for girl. But in his excitement at hearing the Britisher giving words in *Romanes,* as he supposed, and telling how it was spoken by millions of people in India, Boswell broke into a torrent of gypsy, asking what it all meant. This time it was the Englishman's turn to be surprised. Our words had a familiar sound. They surely were intended to be Hindustani; and yet he could not make them out. Glancing at us with contempt, he remarked, "Aw, wye don't you speak the bloody langwidge *right!*"

While living in the same city I gave several talks on the gypsies. After the first I was very much worried at finding it reported in the next morning's paper. What if Johnston's attention should be called to it and he should find out that I was betraying state secrets? It was with fear and trembling that I went to see him a little later. However, after the second talk, as no one had shown him the article, I ceased to worry. Some days after the last, the account of which was very much garbled in one of the newspapers, making the Romanies arch villains, I called on my friend. He received me coolly, but I still was unsuspecting until he produced the paper and ordered me to read the article.

I could feel wave on wave of suppressed anger ready to spring out if I betrayed that I was indirectly responsible for these calumnies against the race. Doing my best to express unconcern, my lips read the words, though my mind was racing from thought to thought in an agony of suspense. Finally I stopped without finishing it. The strain was too great. Assuming a bored air, I handed the paper back to him without remarks, as though I considered the opinions of a *Gajo* beneath further notice. His suspicions were allayed, but I have never ceased to feel re-

morse at not having confessed the real truth of
the matter.

Among most gypsies it is the merry, impish
children that fascinate me most; but among the
Anglo-American Romanies it is the old people.
An elderly gypsy whom I found even more delightful than Johnston Boswell was Sybil Yerne,
Nick's mother, the *tači* [true] Romani *dai* who
had married a Quaker. Nick worshiped her,
and had talked to me about her so often that I
longed to meet her. I was not disappointed.
Deeply in love with her husband, she had become
a house dweller for his sake; but as she advanced
in years the call of the road had grown too strong
and the habits of youth carried her afield. One
day I met her with her son in his camp hundreds
of miles from her home. In spite of her dark
complexion, you would have taken her for a
mild-mannered, motherly Englishwoman—unless
you addressed her in gypsy. If you did, you
would see a roguish flicker in her brown eyes and
hear her say things quite un-Quakerish.

"Aunt Sibi," as the other Romanies called her,
was a true *dŭkkerer*. She herself believed in her
strange powers of divination. "Fortune telling
is a gift," she once said to me. And Mrs. Yerne
was certainly gifted. Sweet and lovable as she
was, she had the reputation of being a bit of a
witch, and none of the gypsies cared to provoke
her anger. She was as wise as a serpent and as

naïve as a child. The human heart was as clear to her as the crystal ball she carried to impress the *Gajos*. Her advice in human affairs was better than that of a Solomon; but her ideas of the material world were rudimentary. She had traveled many thousands of miles, but the earth had simply been a great, moving panorama.

"Don't you think the world is soon comin' to an end?" she asked me one day. When I inquired her reasons for thinking so, she replied, "It's these hautomobiles." They seemed to her positively apocalyptic. Her chief consolation was the hope that gasoline would soon give out.

In describing things, she had the vividness of most gypsies, and her words were often beautiful. She spoke of the joys of wandering in rural England, and occasionally she would sigh for the baked *hočiwiči* [hedgehog], snail soup, pokeweed, and "mushrooms"; but mostly she regretted the beauty of the old cathedrals and the roads across the downs, "with the primroses in the hedges all in clusters."

In the following years I saw her often, and she and Nick would ask me to let them know before they started out each spring, so that they could be prepared to take me with them in their travels in tent and caravan. What a chance I missed! It was not until some years later that I was to share the daily life and constant roamings of the wayward gypsy.

[183]

CHAPTER VII

"WHEN GYPSY FIDDLES CRY"

THE guests were arriving for the wedding. The gypsy orchestra stationed near the door of the hall played the Polish march of welcome as they entered singly or in groups. Gabor, the leader, planted himself in the doorway with his violin, and kept his keen eyes fixed on each arrival until given his present for the music. From the exact depth of his salaam the other players could calculate within a few cents the amount of the tip. Once Gabor failed to bow in the slightest, and eyed with anger and contempt a single nickel in the palm of his hand. Then he hurled it at the guest, who was hurrying away, hoping no one would notice. It struck him in his starched collar. He turned his head with a pained, embarrassed look, and increased his pace. The gypsies muttered an assortment of choice maledictions on the entire Gentile race. A nickel! What an insult to an artist! The coin lay there on the floor until finally a group of children pounced on it with cries of glee.

The hall was a typical institution of the dis-

[184]

trict where the East Side of New York reproduces in miniature the blending of the many races in eastern Europe. It enabled families who lived most of their lives crowded into two or three rooms to have at their disposal, on occasions such as this wedding, a veritable palace with a banquet room, a bowling alley, a ballroom, and a barroom. There was space for all their friends: the dwellers of the street where they lived, the congregation of the church they attended, their fellow factory workers, and their numerous children. And all could do as they fancied. For people whose incomes were figured on the hour-and-penny scale such epic hospitality was possible only through co-operation; but it gave an opportunity for a riotous enjoyment of life. What a contrast to weddings in other classes of American society, where they are simple ceremonies to be consummated with the least possible fuss, or formal affairs in which the amount of boredom is in ratio to the number of guests.

A substantial feast of stuffed cabbage and other delicacies capped with slivovitz, distilled from plums, was spread on long tables each of which seated a hundred people. When all the guests were well filled, and well cheered from the beer that flowed from fifty large pitchers requisitioned from washstands, the plate was passed and the collection taken up to defray expenses.

The bride was Polish, and the groom Russian,

and, although the orchestra was Hungarian gypsy, it played the national dances of the couple at the ball which followed. The gypsies only needed to hear an air once to be able to reproduce it again. There were polkas and mazurkas, whirling waltzes and Russian dances. The music of one of these was wild and barbaric, with a certain Oriental quality. The gypsies themselves were carried away by their music. The dancers forgot everything save the dance, in an ecstasy of motion. Faster and faster it went until only the best and strongest remained, spinning like tops, or like dervishes, in a mad trance.

Gazing on all this merriment, from my seat beside Mirishka, the cembalo player, it was pleasant to think that perhaps I had helped bring the couple together. Two months before, while visiting the gypsies, the bride had entered and had asked to have her fortune told. Since they were musicians and had forgotten the black art, I was called upon to read her palm. Of course I could tell her very little; but she told me a great deal—without knowing it. It was obvious that she was torn between two desires—to marry a man whom she loved, and another who was relatively prosperous. Being romantically inclined, I predicted that she would marry the former—and she did. My words had evidently made an impression, for she told the gypsies to be sure and see that I came to the wedding; and that night she came across the banquet hall to greet me, beaming with joy.

My first meeting with these musicians was characteristic of Romani life. On coming to New York for a year of study, my first move was to go in quest of gypsies. On Avenue B, a few blocks from Little Hungary, I found a gypsy family. In order to avoid the suffocating heat of that September night, they were sitting on the pavement in front of the tenement where they lived. My knowledge of the Hungarian gypsy dialect was limited at that time, and Gabor was not at all impressed by my claim that I was "one of the blood."

However, I had found Romanies, and was not to be rebuffed so easily. In spite of his gruffness, I asked him to have a drink. He refused. The dear old villain loved his glass, but he was too proud to drink with a *Gajo,* an outsider, and a *Gajo* he still believed me to be. Turning to his son, Laioš, a boy about seventeen, I invited him to join me in the corner café; but taking his father's cue he replied that he drank nothing but champagne. The truth was that he never drank at all. Here was my chance. "Very well," I answered, "nothing but champagne it will be."

It was a glorious celebration. Most of the money I had to live on for a month disappeared down thirsty throats; and poor Laioš, little suspecting the potent effect of Piper Heidsieck brut, had to be helped to bed. Before that stage had arrived, however, we were all exceedingly merry. Even the barefooted mother left the tenement and joined us; and the oldest two girls, Panna and Mirishka, whose spirits were naturally exuberant, found an added gayety in the golden bubbles of the wine of France. As they were all musicians, we did not lack entertainment; and my favorite airs were played, together with many wild gypsy melodies.

My knowledge of Nomad gypsy made it possible to understand them fairly well, and we soon became fast friends, so friendly, in fact, that the following morning Gabor took me aside and asked me if I would like to marry one of his daughters.

They were an interesting family. Gabor had been a tent gypsy in Hungary, a horse trader and blacksmith by trade, and an excellent musician by choice. He was short, but strong as a bull, and not unlike one in temperament, though he really had a warm heart.

Laioš was the oldest of ten children, and a remarkable first violin. He was slender, with something of the panther in his make-up. Mirishka, the oldest daughter, had less fire, but was a good cembalo player, and was always smiling. She had a larger dose of quiet common sense than most Romanies; whereas her sister,

Panna, was more like the boy, more feline, more inspired. Another sister was Sarah, who made artificial roses and was a typical product of the East Side. There seemed to be nothing of the Romani in her; but she was extremely good natured and the mainstay of her parents. The tenement consisted of two alcoves the size of a bed, a kitchen barely wide enough for the sink and a stove, end to end, and the fire escape, which was ice-box, balcony, and sleeping porch all in one. It was close quarters for twelve people, but such was their sense of hospitality that they insisted that I spend the night with them. I was given the guest room, or kitchen, the only room that admitted of much privacy. A broken-down cot that left my feet suspended in midair was set up for me under the sink.

Living in such narrow limits has its inconveniences, but it has its joys and its amusing sides. A friend of mine once read in a newspaper that a large family of gypsies in Rochester were said to be living with no furniture save one chair, one bed, and a bathtub; and he asked if it really could be true. As a matter of fact it was surprising that they had so much—especially a bathtub. But Gabor, too, had one. It had been prescribed by the doctor. As it was a great curiosity, the entire family and an occasional neighbor or two would gather around the tub to see him use it; and being a modest man, whenever he bathed he kept his underwear on.

As for the joys of tenement life, they were chiefly in the friendly gatherings. The natural gayety of the Romanies made their little living room attractive to the entire neighborhood, and sometimes a few *Gajos* were admitted. One of these privileged persons was a young violin mender from Vienna. Another was a waiter from Galicia. Both had had the advantages of the excellent Austrian system of high-school education; and on one occasion they had a heated debate over some point in Greek versification. It nearly ended in a fist fight. Each was soothed, however, by the approval of the other as they cited verses from Homer in the original.

The waiter came from a family of well-to-do brewers in Lemberg. He had been engaged to a girl by parental arrangement, at the age of seventeen. The girl was a pianist, and apparently was not delighted with the plan, for one day when she was playing and he complimented her, she replied, "What do you know about music?" He was so nettled that he ran away to America. The East Side had taught him English and manners that were anything but elegant; but he still preserved a sensitive soul. He was too retiring, in fact, to be a fortunate lover. His affections were never requited.

"Lizzie no like me," he related one evening.

"And for her I lose twenty pounds of fat. I get so nervous I break too many dishes at the hotel, and de boss he take five dollars off my wages. I t'ink about her so hard dat one day I spill a plate of noodles down a gentleman's collar."

But worst of all was his unhappy love for Jane. The girl had been fond of him, and in order to show his undying affection he had had tattooed on his arm, "Jane. Yours forever." Alas! Jane's older sister had not approved of the waiter and had forbidden her to see him again. "And dat girl she lufe me so little she gife up to her sister. And now I'm crazy about anoder girl, but I can't get dat damn 'Jane. Yours forever,' off my arm, and I'm scared to hell my girl she see it."

If there was much that was entertaining, there was even more that was beautiful. Never shall I forget the first morning, when I awoke there— awoke on my broken cot under the sink. The Piper Heidsieck contained no headache, and its effect was remarkably persistent. Gradually I emerged from the realms of dream to the accompaniment of strains of weird and lovely music. Consciousness slowly came,

"Like a black panther from the caves of sleep."

The melody reached me in a twilight state, somewhere beyond time and space, and I floated with it until I awoke.

It was then I found the source of the music.

"In a vision once I saw
A damsel with a dulcimer."

Panna, the romantic, was in fact playing a dulcimer, or cembalo. She was learning an ancient song, repeating the melody on the instrument as her father played it on his violin. Thus it had been handed down from generation to generation of gypsies.

Here was a song that contained the very essence of life—its deep, intangible emotions. Perhaps the elements of it went back to the days when the Romanies still wandered in India; and yet each succeeding player had put something of his own soul into the music. Never having been fixed on paper, it had never grown rigid, though it was far from formless.

Panna was putting into the notes all her suppressed longings, her eager, budding womanhood, her awakening senses, and timid fears. The father was passing on to her the sacred cup of skill and knowledge, and she was filling it with all her youth. The scene enabled me to understand, as I never had before, the closing stanza of Sarojni Naida's "The Indian Gypsy":

"Time's river winds in foaming centuries
Its changing, swift, irrevocable course
To far-off and incalculable seas;
She is twin-born with primal mysteries,
And drinks of life at Time's forgotten source."

[192]

"WHEN GYPSY FIDDLES CRY"

There have been many futile controversies among musicians in regard to Hungarian gypsy music. Is it Hungarian or is it gypsy? Some twenty years ago Bartok Bela and Kodaly Zoltan, two distinguished Magyar composers, traveled throughout Hungary, recording folksongs. Their collection had various important results, one of which was to prove that "Hungarian folk-music and gypsy music are by no means the same." Moreover, one has only to notice the striking similarity of the airs played by the gypsies of Hungary, Russia, and Rumania to be convinced that most decidedly there is such a thing as genuine Romani music.

Tradition has it that about A.D. 420 a thousand Luris, gypsy minstrels, male and female, were sent from India to the Shah of Persia; and the presence to-day of wandering gypsy-like musicians in Iran, who bear the same name and conform to the descriptions of them in an old poem, seems to substantiate the tradition. If true, this was the first gypsy migration from India. But whether true or not, it is a fact that the occupations of metal-working and music are the most typical ones practiced by Romani men, as fortune telling, music, and dancing are those of the women.

The arts of music and dancing were more or less lost in the countries which were not in a position to understand their peculiar style, which was wholly Oriental. This is particularly true of the British Isles; and yet we know that a group of gypsies danced and sang before King James in Holyrood Palace; and does not Johnston Boswell claim that his father was "the best fiddler in Canady." In Paris I once heard a French Romani improvise a remarkable accompaniment on the guitar to Massenet's *"Meditation de Thaïs,"* which he had never before even heard.

In Russia, previous to the revolution, men of nobility and wealth paid fabulous sums to the gypsy singers and dancers. Their music is more stimulating than wine, to the extent of becoming a dangerous passion, exemplifying in reality the legend of Homer's sirens. Those who have read *The Brothers Karamazov,* or Tolstoy's *Redemption,* will have a faint perception of this fact, though only those who have seen and heard them can realize it completely.

Catalini, the celebrated Italian singer of some seventy-five years ago, on hearing a Russian gypsy songstress, tore from her own shoulders the splendid cashmere shawl which the Pope had given her as a matchless singer, saying, as she handed it to the tzigane, "I have met an artist who is more than my match."

In Poland, in Bohemia, in all the Balkans, and in Turkey the music of the gypsies is highly esteemed by the cultivated and uncultivated alike. They are the principal musicians of the

[194]

people, for in these countries there was a sufficient Oriental influence to make their music intelligible. In Spain it was the same, and the
wealth of semi-Eastern music preserved in that
country by the Gitanos is just beginning to be
adequately used by the composers. Only now is
the West fully awakening to the beauty of
Oriental art.

The similarity of gypsy songs to those of India
is striking: the peculiar intervals, half and quarter tones, the "curves of sound," more important
than the quality of the tone, the frequency of
grace notes, the "extemporizing according to
rule," the long pauses during which the listener
"hangs upon the player."

Similar analogies between gypsy dances and
those of India might also be pointed out.

Though the gypsies of India to-day are musicians, nowhere have they attained such perfection
as in the land of the Magyars, where their
favorite instrument is the violin.

No one knows just where and when the violin
was evolved. The ancestor of this instrument
doubtless came, like the Romanies, from India.
There is a bare possibility that they brought it
with them into Europe. A Romani legend ex-
plains its origin.

There was once a maiden so hopelessly in love
that she invoked the devil's aid. The Evil One
promised to help her if she would give him her

four brothers and her parents. Much as she loved
them, she loved the youth even more, and so she
yielded them to the devil. As they slept he made
of the father a box, of the mother a bow, and of
the brothers he made four strings. The devil
then taught her how to play this new instrument
—the violin; and with it she won the heart of her
lover. But Satan came and seized them both,
and the violin was left lying in the forest. A
poor gypsy came by and saw it. He played, and
as he played in town and hamlet all men laughed
or wept as he chose.

It is literally true that the Romanies with their
songs have been able to do just that—make men
laugh and weep. Baudelaire did not mention the
gypsies in his prose poem, *"Les Vocations,"* but
he certainly had them in mind when he said:
"They were tall, and though in rags very proud,
with an air of being dependent on no man.
Their eyes actually shone as they played their
music, music so astonishing that now it made you
want to dance, now to weep, now to do both at
the same time; and it seemed as though you
would go mad if you listened too long a time."

Gypsy music is an expression of the depths of
gloom and crests of joy between which the
Romani spirit flies on swift wings. It is always
passionate, even when most graceful. It has a
largeness that suggests the joys and sorrows of
the universe, rather than of the individual. It is

elemental like the mountains and the sea. The fiercely proud and pleasure-loving Magyar and the mystic, exalted Slav have found a voice in gypsy violins.

It seems strange that these airs which you hear at balls and weddings on the East Side of New York, and in the gay cafés of Budapest and voluptuous Bukharest should contain such an ocean of hidden, inexpressible sadness, such infinite world-weariness. But the songs are never sad for long. Invariably they are followed by airs that incite a sudden whirlwind of energy or a breathless impulse to dance.

Strange, too, is the seeming lack of variety and the Oriental ornateness of these songs, at least for the Western ear, accustomed to more melody. The solution of the enigma is given by Liszt; and it is important because it is the key to much of his own work, which, in the hands of the average virtuoso, often seems mere flourish: "In gypsy art the multiplicity of musical arabesques that are played between all the motifs, no matter what their character, forms a sort of dense foliage of bright colors, constantly rustling and stirring, at the roots of which lie the deep emotions, like great birds shyly moving among the thorny bushes in full bloom."

The unit of the Hungarian gypsy orchestra is the string quartette with the addition of the cembalo, which is like a small square piano with the strings exposed. It is descended from the psaltery of the Bible and is the ancestor of the pianoforte. The strings are struck with slender batons, the ends of which are tightly wrapped with thread. To be sure, its tone is sweet, as the name dulcimer implies, but its dominant qualities are strength and vibrancy.

The first violin carries the melody, while the others, and especially the cembalo, build a towering mass of harmony like the blossoms and leafage that completely envelop the central trunk and branches of certain tropical trees. The first violin is the leader. The others simply follow. The music is never written; and the leader will often elaborate the theme according to the inspiration of the moment.

Gypsy music has had an important influence on some of the chief composers, from Haydn, whose "Gypsy Rondo" has but little of the Romani fire, through Beethoven, Schubert, Berlioz, Brahms, and Dvořák, down to the contemporary Rumanian composer, Enescu, whose "Rhapsodies" are saturated with gypsy feeling. But the man whose compositions are most akin to those of these roamers is Liszt.

"Recollections of the gypsies," said the great Hungarian, "are associated with memories of my childhood and some of its most vivid impressions." At the age of eleven he heard the gypsy virtuoso, Bihary, and says of him, "The notes of his bewitching violin fell upon my ear like drops of some fiery, volatile essence." It was the playing of Bihary that definitely determined him to consecrate his entire life to music.

The gypsy airs clung to his imagination, taking deepest root, and fructifying it, he says. More than once he compared himself to the Romanies. He too had been a wanderer in strange lands, pursuing his ideal of art. Returning to his native land, he sought them out in the forest, and, sitting by their camp fires or reclining on a mound of thyme and sweet flowers, he listened to their demoniac playing and watched their wild abandon, storing up themes for his "Hungarian Rhapsodies."

While in Paris in 1840 the composer was presented with a gypsy boy of one of his Magyar friends. The little lad of twelve was slim and tawny, with wildly waving hair, "a bold look, and a demeanor as haughty as though he were to challenge all the kings in the world." He became impetuously fond of Liszt, but in spite of this his insolence, his tendency to steal out of greediness, his desire to hug all the "grandes dames," his reckless disregard for money, and his extraordinary personal vanity made him quite a problem. Civilization was only spoiling him and giving him nothing in return. He was too proud and independent to study in a school, though when Liszt left for Spain he turned him over to the violin professor of the Paris Conservatory, who promised to do his utmost for the lad's astonishing musical talent.

It was useless. Like a genuine savage, he was interested only in *his own* pleasures, *his own* violin, and *his own* music. Willingly and with remarkable surety and vigor he would play the ·liveliest czardas, but the melodies he heard at the Conservatory seemed to him dull and insipid. Finally, seeing that he had undertaken a hopeless task, Liszt restored him to his brothers, whom he happened to meet in Vienna. The boy's rapture on meeting them was so boundless that they feared he would go mad. With expressions of passionate gratitude he begged Liszt to be allowed to return at once and forever to his own people. No sooner were they reunited than the band disappeared from the city to show the lost child to his father.

Liszt and his friends had filled the haughty little fellow's purse with contributions which were squandered immediately on a colossal banquet for his brothers.

Liszt's relation to the Romanies is well known, but that of Schubert, and the master of masters, Beethoven, though important, has scarcely been pointed out. I had always felt that there was a passionate quality in Beethoven's music, which was lacking in that of Mozart and Bach, and in that of his predecessors. There is a chasm-like depth to his expression of the tragic emotions and a fierce intensity in his joy, witness the Scherzo of the Ninth Symphony, quite different from Bach's bonhomie and serene gayety. There are sudden transitions in the works of Beethoven unlike anything save those of gypsy music. Though the tziganes taught him little directly, indirectly they showed him the value of spontaneity, which led him to express his tumultuous spirit in rhapsodic bursts of feeling, which shocked his less romantic contemporaries.

Imagine my delight on learning that the master's patron, Esterhazy, had a gypsy orchestra, and on recognizing a definitely gypsy theme in the "King Stephen Overture"! Later I learned that he had taken this theme from Bihary, whose playing had thrilled him as it had Liszt. Later still I came on these lines in Liszt's rare and beautiful book, *Des Bohémiens et de leur Musique,* speaking of gypsy music: "Beethoven was acquainted with it, as is obvious from more than one of his pages . . . more than one of his ideas . . . more than one of the daring flights in his later works!"

As for Schubert, I heard an interesting anecdote in this regard from the American composer, Edgar Stillman Kelly. He had heard it some years ago from an aged musician in Switzerland, who had heard it from Schubert himself. It has never been published.

Schubert had been invited to the Esterhazy country estate in Hungary, and, being too poor to take the stage-coach, he had walked. On the way he met a band of gypsies, and, captivated by their music, he spent two days with them. Appreciating his mastery of music, his genius, and his friendly, Bohemian nature, they had received him gladly. Suddenly remembering his engagement with the Esterhazys, he was ashamed to appear so late, and stayed with the gypsy band for the entire summer. As a result we have the "Fantaisie Hongroise," the "Moment Musical," in which one can fairly see the Romanies leaping and dancing about their camp fire, and lastly a theme in one of his rarely played but most beautiful symphonies.

There is a bond of fellow feeling between the unknown gypsy fiddlers and the famous artists which is striking. A Romani tough, a hanger-on at pool halls, who asked me to feel a scar on his head from a knife duel, told me that he had spent his last two dollars to hear the Boston Symphony under Muck. On another occasion a gypsy who played in a moving-picture theater in Pittsburgh gave me a keenly discriminating analysis of the art of the great Ysaye, adding that he felt the Belgian was the most noble and poetic of violinists: *"Leski lavutar jilabel"* ("His violin sings").

Only a few years ago, when Ysaye was on tour

with the Cincinnati Orchestra, he accepted the invitation of a gypsy to partake of the good cheer of his humble house. A friend who was present told me that the master played for him, and the gypsy was highly appreciative; but like Liszt's protégé, he regarded Romani music more highly than aught else, and played a czardas for Ysaye, asking him if he could do the same. The great violinist with his large good-nature accepted the challenge, but no sooner had he executed a few measures than the tzigane snatched the violin from his hands, saying, "That's no way!" and finished the piece with gusto, much to the amusement of the master.

Kubelik esteems the gypsies highly when they play their own compositions; and an Australian singer who paid him a visit at his country estate in Bohemia told me that he had invited a gypsy band to serenade his guests Christmas morning.

Both in Europe and in America most of the gypsy musicians are house-dwellers, and often settle down in large cities; but frequently the roving spirit is roused, and they long for the great tent of clouds and blue sky. Sometimes the wild beasts born in cages seem to pine for the open even more than their sires who were captured in the jungle; and often the city-born children of tent-dwellers will leave their parents, despite the strength of Romani blood ties.

Several months after meeting Gabor's family in New York, I took a tiny garret room in Eighth Street near Sixth Avenue, which overlooked a sea of roofs, the lighted cross on Washington Square, and the distant tower of the Woolworth Building. The view was its one attraction.

About two o'clock one morning I was still at work on some poems of Leconte de Lisle. Outside, a wintry rain was beating against the windows; inside, the dingy walls had disappeared before visions of Brahma, and of a thousand virgins in a Himalayan lake. I had just gone to bed when, without warning, some one rapped long and sharply on my door. No one had ever visited me before at any hour in my cell. Who could it be?

As I lighted the gas the door swung open, and there stood Laioš, his black hair glistening with the rain, his violin case under his damp coat, closely hugged to his breast. He had run away from home and had been wandering alone for days.

First he had fled to the house of some gypsy musicians in another town; but, finding the man working in a factory, he had come away at once, his spirit of independence overcoming his hunger. "Just imagine," he said to me, "a gypsy and an artist working like that!" And so he had come to me.

On certain afternoons and evenings I was

studying at Columbia; but during the three days
he stayed with me I adroitly managed so that
he would not catch me at anything so ungypsy
as work. My irregular comings and goings had
a Romani-like mysteriousness. Like all well-
bred people, gypsies do not pry too closely into
one another's affairs—for obvious reasons! He
might have thought that I was a crook, but at
least he did not take me for a wage-slave.

Among the Paris students there is a saying
that the month—meaning the monthly allowance
—ends on the fifth. And it was after the fifth.
As for a bed, although even the gypsy com-
plained of the narrowness and hardness of mine,
the problem was solved; but food was another
matter. It was difficult enough to provide myself with a sufficient supply of black olives, rich,
oily, and cheap, and with bread to keep myself
going; but it would have been still harder to feed
a growing boy.

The next night we started out to make some
money. I introduced Laioš to the charming
Irishman who ran the near-by saloon where
Masefield had once been a porter, and who now
reads Masefield's verse with delight. But gypsy
music was not a commodity he needed at the
time. In an Italian saloon on Eighth Street the
Romani fiddled "O Sole Mio," and I passed the
hat. It yielded only a nickel. "Get something

new!" a Neapolitan advised. "That old stuff
makes my head ache."

From there we sought out a German bar on
Irving Place. It was the year before the United
States entered the war, and German patriotism
ran high and unrestrained. According to a pre-
concerted plan, we entered separately and sat
down at the same table without greeting each
other. Casually I asked Laioš if that was a
fiddle he had in the case, and suggested that he
play something. "Give us the *Wacht am
Rhein!*" I called loudly. When he finished it
he was applauded. I asked for his cap and,
ostentatiously putting a quarter in it myself, I
passed it around. Dimes and nickels rained, and
one good patriot under whose nose I let drop
the quarter, reluctantly followed my example,
saying, as he held the coin a few moments in his
fingers, "It's a lot of money!"

Thus we managed to exist until Laioš finally
decided to return to his family. The songbird
had lived too long in a cage.

The reason he had run away was both pathetic
and amusing. It was during Lent, which is a
period of involuntary fasting among most gypsy
muscians who make their hand-to-mouth living
playing for balls and weddings. Everything had
been pawned. They were almost starving. It
was then that the father thought of a ruse. He
belonged to a mutual insurance society that paid

its members a fixed sum each week that they were incapacitated by illness. I had been mystified by the fact that Gabor had been sick each time I had called at the tenement, and that on seeing me he had always gotten up, suddenly and miraculously cured.

After spending two weeks in bed the monotony of it had palled on his gypsy spirit, and he had gone to the headquarters of the society to collect his money. Guessing the trick, but having no proof of it, the agent paid him, saying, "It's the last time we'll take a gypsy!" Enraged at the insult to his race, Gabor gathered his Romani friends together and got uproariously drunk. Coming home penniless, he was so ashamed that, in order to rehabilitate himself in his own eyes, he beat his wife.

That same year in New York I met one of the best known Hungarian gypsy musicians, Rigo Yansci. He was playing at Allaire's on Third Avenue, after having played before the highest aristocracy of Europe. His features were almost ugly, but the charm of his personality was great. His manner drew the crowd to him exactly as the coils of a dynamo make the heavy wheel spin round. The people in the crowded hall all but fought for the privilege of having him sit at their tables and drink Rigo cocktails with them. In his early days Queen Victoria had been pleased to shake hands with him; and as he told me about it he chuckled over her patronizing manner.

In later years the Princess de Chimay, the daughter of an American millionaire, had been captivated by Rigo's playing and his magnetism, and had run away with him, proving again the truth of Wilde's statement that art does not imitate nature, but nature art. More than once the nobility of various countries have followed the example of the high-born lady in the old ballad of Johnie Faa:

> "The gypsies came to our good lord's gate,
> And, ah, but they sang sweetly!
> They sang so sweet and so complete
> That down came the fair lady."

She yields to the gypsy's plea to come with him, and throws off her fine mantle, saying:

> "For if kith and kin and all had sworn,
> I'll follow the gypsy laddie."

Some years later I saw him playing in Little Hungary. Illness, age, and too many Rigo cocktails had dimmed his luster. He had just finished playing a beautiful czardas amid the din of voices, the clink of ice in glasses, the bustling of waiters, and the half-drunken shouts of would-be Bohemians who were paying little heed to the rare melody. *"Mro čavo* [my boy]," he said to me, sadly offering me a cigarette from a gold case given him by a Russian grand duke, "what do they care for music?" But I knew he was thinking, "My star has set!"

A gypsy must be young to play his best: it is so much a matter of passion and temperament. This is their tragedy. When they have mastered their technique and acquired a large repertory— it is sometimes too late. There was a world of pathos in the words of Gabor, when he said to me once, *"Som p'uro!"* ('I am old!") No wonder gypsy music is the gayest and the saddest in the world!

When last I saw Rigo he was playing in a little café on First Avenue, tawdry with cheap artificial flowers. It was almost deserted. Rigo himself limped painfully like a wounded stag; but when he played, one's only impression was one of mastery and of fascination. And when he sat down, he laughed and smiled with unfailing youthfulness, though there was no one on whom to exercise his charm save a drunken Slovak. Just once did he show any sadness. For a moment his eyes glistened with tears when another violinist played an air with which he had captivated the women of two continents.

Rigo is by no means the only tzigane who has become internationally famous as a musician. There is Boldi, whose name for years shone in electric lights on the most frequented spot on the globe: the corner of the Café de La Paix where the Place de l'Opéra joins the Grand Boulevard.

There is Racz Laczi, one of the most extraordinary violinists I have ever heard. On arriving in Budapest last summer one of the first things that caught my attention was a long paper ribbon pasted on the window of a coffee house, announcing in large letters in Magyar, "Racz Laczi, King of musicians, and his son, the Prince of players," a very royal combination, as indeed it proved. Laczi reminded me of nothing so much as a Bengal tiger, so colorful, so powerful, and at times so delicate and softly graceful was his playing. But he is only one of thirty-two sons, all well-known musicians. His brother Pal, with whom I struck up a sort of father-and-son friendship while in Budapest, had been equally, if not more, famous in his day.

In the coffee house where I met him nightly, in the Prater Street, where only gypsies were admitted from two in the morning until eight, I was told by the tzigane who had charge of finding positions for the musicians that there were about six hundred gypsy bands in Budapest alone at that moment. It was not hard to believe, for at six o'clock one morning I counted some three hundred Romanies in that one café.

In New York there are not a few places where you may find them. There are two full-blooded gypsies in the Biltmore orchestra, who speak

Romanes beautifully. There are little cafés in the Hungarian quarters on the East Side where one may hear most unusual Romani music. In Sixth Street there was formerly a bar run by a gypsy violinist, Zambory, where I spent many a joyous evening. One of the most characteristic places was the Rakoczy, a dining and drinking hall that opened off a bar. Prohibition, alas! has closed its doors.

The leader was Louis Bogar, a thorough musician with a quiet, gentlemanly manner and a certain naïve quality, beneath which lay the old gypsy fire. Save a few writers and painters, no one came there save the Hungarians of the neighborhood. The note of false Bohemianism was carefully excluded—but such gayety! Louis would sip his white wine, well *gespritzt,* or a glass of genuine Tokay, and tell us of his past triumphs and of his thirty-odd hats, one of which cost him forty dollars. Occasionally we would try to dance a czardas, to the amusement of the habitués.

Not even in Hungary have I seen people as deeply affected by gypsy music as at the Rackoczy. The slow lassan would begin. Every ear would be attention. Sometimes Bogar's quick eye would see that some man was in a mood to sing and, approaching his table, he would "play in his ear," with muted strings. The fellow's head would be thrown high, his right arm stretched upward in passionate gestures, and with a full throat he would pour out his heart, while the gypsy orchestra would sound the depths of tragedy, with chords so wild and sweet that more than once I have seen stalwart workmen weep.

The lassan would be followed by a movement somewhat faster, in which notes of momentary despair would blend into transports of swift joy, like rose petals hurled on the wings of a June thunderstorm. This would be followed in turn by the rapid dance movement, the frishka, in which gayety would be carried to the verge of delirium, and pleasure to the point of paroxysm.

The songs of well-known poets, such as those of the great Petöfi, have sometimes been sung to these melodies. Often the words are folk songs and are themselves very old. Here is a translation of a characteristic song by an unknown singer, crude but not inexpressive, which is sometimes sung to the lassan, the slow movement:

> "Play on, gypsy, till her heart
> Break as mine shall when we part!
> Make the four strings quiver, moan,
> Cry as I shall cry—alone!
> Make the four strings quiver, moan,
> Cry as I shall cry—alone!"

Another beautiful gypsy song is "Far and High the Cranes Give Cry." It contains an expression of ineffable yearning.

To illustrate the character of the words sung to the second movement let me give a song I learned from a gypsy in Transylvania, which he sang for me in Romani. Recently I also heard it sung by a Nomad gypsy coppersmith in France; and it vaguely recalls one of Leland's gypsy songs.

> *"Pal o pani ov pirel;*
> *"Mro pirano bašavel!*
> *Vakren dui kale yaka:*
> *—Mikliom mira gulva da!"*

> ("'Cross the brook his footsteps stray;
> Hear my darling lover play!
> Dark eyes whisper as they shine:
> —Thus I left sweet mother mine!")

In 1922 I met some gypsy musicians in Vienna who were practically starving; but they made a jest of the condition, and in playing the frishka they sang the following words:

> "'Nanai maro, nanai mas,
> Nanai buko balovas . . .'"

> ("'We've no bread, and we've no meat,
> We've no tripe that we can eat . . .'")

I saw to it that the next day they had both bread and meat.

I have met wandering gypsy bands in many American cities. In half a dozen towns they re-side permanently. It is from Cleveland that the Princess Veronica starts on her tours, playing the cembalo as a headliner in vaudeville. In Chicago there are both Hungarian and Rumanian gypsy musicians. There they play for the working classes, in the humblest of saloons, the same music that their fellow Romanies play in the smartest night cafés of Montmartre to-day.

In my quest of gypsy music in Chicago I once wandered into a Rumanian ball that was being given above a saloon somewhere on Milwaukee Avenue. The dancers were dressed in their beautiful Vlach costumes, as colorful as any in Europe; and with characteristic Rumanian love of pleasure they were abandoning themselves to the stormy merriment of the tzigane melodies.

Some time ago while on my way from Chicago to New York I looked out of the car window near Pittsburgh and noticed that the station was Braddock. Remembering that a Romani had told me that there was a big gypsy settlement there, I jumped off the train and went in search of it. Near the depot I found some forty or fifty families living in shanties grouped about a sort of square. In the background rose row on row of huge stacks from grimy smelters, rolling out billows of smoke that hung in the air above us. Nothing daunted the gypsies' spirits, however. After greeting me as brother, they arranged an entertainment. A table was spread in the open,

A youthful piper

with enough to drink to make the whole colony merry, and a large orchestra was immediately improvised, with two cembalos set back to back.

And there, while the yellow smoke from the stacks poured out in ghastly clouds, shutting out the blue sky, they played their wonderful weird music, forgetting everything in the exaltation of their art.

When night fell and the pall of smoke was tinged a lurid red, and great tongues of flame shot forth from the smelters, they were still playing. Fumes of wine were in their blood now, as well as the madness of the music; and they played the final movements of the czardas like demons, but they played the plaintive parts with even greater tenderness than before, and a deeper spirit of yearning.

From Braddock they go to various points where they find Rumanians, Magyars, and Slovaks, who work chiefly in the steel mills and to whom the gypsy music is a great boon. I have seen them in queer little bars listening to it with a fierce joy, after a day spent in the grime, the din, and the terrible heat of the rolling mills and blast furnaces. It rouses and sustains them, as it sustained their ancestors in the gloomiest hours of Turkish domination. In their native lands they are mostly pastoral peoples, and the gypsy strains must bring them visions of mountain torrents, white with foam, dashing down hillsides, or the young wheat of the Pussa, the great green plain of Hungary, tossing in the wind.

As I write this I am staying with friends in the heart of Cincinnati, who are the sort of hosts one likes to imagine but seldom finds. From the open porch, roofed with green leaves, one overlooks the Ohio. On either side is a ravine, from which rise lofty trees that frame the view. Below the deep sloping lawn they join in an emerald fringe that hides the railroad tracks along the river bank. The curving branch of an ancient ash, just beyond the porch, sounds the theme, repeated in the curves of the Kentucky hills, a symphony of line and color. There are countless shades of green. There are many tones of red from the houses on the opposite bank, softening to rose by the distance and a vague mist. At twilight the milk-and-coffee color of the broad stream turns to a mellow olive. A crimson canoe, catching the last rays of the sun, gives the one touch of brilliant color that was lacking. The scene is now as beautiful as the Bosphorus.

Everything is perfect here; but the June foliage, the song of the birds, and a half-remembered gypsy air are calling to me to join the Romanies. The leaves of a poplar branch beside my window are shaking in the breeze like a flock of tiny green birds, fluttering their wings, but never flying away.

"WHEN GYPSY FIDDLES CRY"

Soon, instead of writing about the gypsies I shall be living with them, which is better. Soon I shall be sitting by gypsy fires and hear the old melodies. Soon I shall be once more on the never-ending trail.

CHAPTER VIII

THE NEVER-ENDING TRAIL

ALL winter I had been dreaming of this: a tent in a gypsy camp, a tent of my own, where I could be the host.

Spring had come late this year, and, had it come early, it would have done me little good, so confining were those last few months of work. Toward the end, when splendid weather came and I had been able to take an occasional half day off for auto rides and picnics, the joy of it had only deepened the longing to join the gypsies, to make every day a holiday, and life itself a picnic.

When I awoke, the rain was pattering on the brown canvas overhead, a sleepy music that made me roll over in the soft eiderdown *šeran* and fall into a long drowse. The pleasure of utter relaxation penetrated that state in which one is just sufficiently conscious to realize that one is asleep and dreaming.

The stopping of the rain awakened me completely. I had only to gather up the big feather bed with its bright-red cover, stack it in a corner, draw on my shoes, and step into the open. Another day of delicious idling and amusement had begun.

The warm June sun had made a hole in the clouds, and was standing well above the straight line of woods on the opposite side of the fields. Tiny drops of water were shining like crystal beads on the clover. The air was sweet and clear. My tent lay at the entrance to the camp in a large grove of oak trees. A vague trail ran along the edge of the grove to the main highway, half a mile away. Each side of this curving woodland lane was bordered with wild roses and purple spider lilies with delicate iris-like blossoms and narrow pointed leaves in graceful clusters— the most beautiful, perhaps, of all our wildflowers.

In the other direction lay the tents, some thirty-five, in oval formation about a clearing separated from the clover field by a narrow fringe of trees. They were all of American make, but some had been designed according to the owners' ideas of beauty in wide strips of alternating red- and orange-colored canvas: "*Romane tsere,*" real gypsy tents, as one of the owners had said. Nearly all of the tents were big enough for a family of seven or eight.

It was the largest camp I have ever seen. Being extremely gregarious, gypsies tend to gather together in units as large as possible, but there are two reasons why large assemblies are rare: first of all, their nomadic occupations are of such a nature that only a few can find work in a given locality at a given time; secondly, the more there are of them the more they are feared.

The chief of the clan was Woršo, whose fortune I had told some years before. He had returned from the exile in Serbia imposed by the United States government, following the quarrel with his son, Stivo, which I had predicted. A compromise had been effected between the two: whenever Woršo was away from the main body of the tribe, Stivo was to rule in his stead.

The various families belonged to the variety of Nomads called Kaldaráš, formerly Coppersmiths, but practising their handicraft only rarely and living almost exclusively on the money made by the women in fortune telling. One family was from Hungary, another from Turkey, another from Russia, and still another from Africa. Woršo and a few others were from Serbia, but most of them were from Greece. Nearly all had been in Argentina, and spoke Spanish as well as English with fluency. Romani was their mother tongue, and they spoke it exclusively among themselves.

It was Sunday, and tapers were burning before the old Byzantine ikons in the tents. This was the extent of their religious devotions. Observance of the religious festivals of the countries

*"Grandma" Stanley, the wife of
one of the former leaders of the
Rumanian gypsies in America*

where they happen to live is felt to bring luck, and gives an excuse for merrymaking. In Constantinople, for instance, the Mohammedan Friday, the Jewish Saturday, and the Christian Sunday bring a welcome series of idle days each week, not to mention the innumerable holy days celebrated by the three religions in the course of the year.

A large group had gathered in the center of the clearing, squatting on their heels, or sitting on the grass, though it was still wet. A fierce debate was taking place. According to the laws of the Nomads in America, who have a very simple but effective government within a government, the quarrel was to be decided by *diwano,* or council, that afternoon, but in the meantime a lively argument was an exciting way of passing the time. Like the Athenians, who spent their leisure moments in brief encounters at arms, in lawsuits, or in parliamentary debates, the gypsies spend long hours in verbal battles which satisfy their combative instincts without a stupid and unnecessary shedding of blood.

To have seen them without understanding the words, one would have thought that they were cursing one another with the utmost venom, and that the next moment knives would be unsheathed and throats slit. A woman with a faint blue tattoo mark just above her chin was talking in so great a rage that her voice rose to such a pitch

[221]

that it continually cracked and broke. From time to time her lips would move breathlessly without emitting a sound, though her rolling eyeballs, waving arms, and swaying body continued to be most articulate. A short, dark man, whose swarthy face was pitted with smallpox, was so incensed by the remarks of one of the debaters that he rolled on the ground like a child, slapping his brow with the palms of both hands.

The subject of the controversy was whether or not the short man should be allowed to leave Cuba with his wife. According to the law, or custom, the payment of a good round sum for a bride by no means constitutes free purchase. After the ceremony the bridegroom, especially if the couple are youthful, must undergo a period of probation during which he is virtually the slave of his father-in-law, obliged to obey him and stay with him until he judges the son-in-law a worthy protector for his daughter. Often the period of probation is merely nominal—the bride's father gives the couple their independence at once. The custom is doubtless to protect the bride, who is often extremely young, and to guard against the possible evils of bride purchase.

In the case of this particular couple they were both about twenty-five, but had not been given their freedom. The girl's father saw that she could not be happy with her husband and was waiting for an opportune moment to secure a separation. The husband, Koina, not only was far from handsome, with his pockmarks, a scar from a knife wound, heavy black stubble on his chin, and with small snaky eyes, but also his character was far from agreeable. He was impulsive and not overintelligent. He was suspicious even of his friends. The girl, Nura, had blue eyes, showing a strain of *Gajo* blood in her ancestry; but her lively temperament was wholly Romani. Koina's projected trip to Cuba was merely an excuse to escape from the father-in-law; and the latter welcomed it as a pretext to obtain a divorce for his daughter before the *diwano*.

Ili, a tall, clever gypsy who had once been the chief, took me aside during the wrangling and told me the situation, adding: "Here is a chance for you to get a bride. The council will be against Koina. They'll give him back most of the money he paid for Nura. He's only been married a couple of weeks. Her father won't be able to get much for her when she marries again. Give me something for arranging it, and I'll see that you get her. You know how it is with us: we don't give our daughters *ivye* [for nothing]. You can't stay long with us unmarried. The fathers are afraid you might run away with one of their girls."

Any objections I could make to his proposal

were met with a torrent of rebuttals. His volubility was too much for me. The only means of putting him off was to say that it was useless to come to a decision before Nura was even separated from her present spouse.

During the afternoon a Packard, a Buick, and two or three smaller cars overflowing with gayly dressed Romanies appeared from another camp and from Chicago, which was only some thirty-five miles distant from our camp beyond Thornton. Some came for the council, others for the usual Sunday festivities, and others merely to visit friends and relatives.

The *diwano* did not take place, owing to the absence of the chief, called away to bail out a woman arrested for palmistry. She had been late in paying blackmail to the police captain in the precinct where she was "working." I was glad of the postponement, for it gave me another week before Ili could bother me with suggestions of marrying Nura.

The wrangling of the morning was forgotten. The sun was shining, but the rain had broken the hot spell and the warm air was languorously caressing—just the right temperature for doing nothing. As the hours passed I wandered from tent to tent, accepting invitations to taste this or that tidbit or drink a glass of wine. There was no regular dinner hour. At varying intervals something was set a-cooking on the triangular three-legged iron in front of each tent: a fowl with tomatoes, onions, sweet peppers, bacon, parsley, and potatoes evolving into a succulent Romani *zumi,* or a juicy sirloin broiling on the charcoal, or a suckling pig slowly browning over the red coals and sending forth odors that moistened the mouths of everyone in the entire camp. Whenever the food was ready anyone was welcome to squat around the sawed-off table or the immense round eating tray, the *skafidi.*

I had given Miloš and his wife, Zaga, money to buy materials for a savory *zumi,* and felt more or less the host in their big striped tent, as various Romanies dropped in, attracted by the subtle blend of ingredients in the steam that rose from the kettle. Even from a distance a whiff of that steam acted as a powerful appetizer even on those who had been regaling themselves with rich morsels half the afternoon.

There were only three plates, in spite of the fact that Miloš had a big family, and only one was a soup plate, which fell to the lot of the host. As the *zumi* in my shallow plate was soon exhausted, Miloš told me to dip into his with my spoon, and, seeing me hesitate, he expostulated, "Don't be ashamed!" I followed his instructions until the entire contents of the kettle was dumped into a huge platter in the center of the hammered copper tray. There were enough spoons to go around, and soon every place was taken by gypsies sitting cross-legged in a ring, and scooping up the contents of the platter or sopping it up with hunks of bread. Breaking a piece from the breast of the tender juicy fowl with his fingers, Miloš fed it to me—an act of friendship and homage.

Having eaten with the gypsies countless times, I felt no squeamishness, for in all essential ways they are cleaner than the majority of *Gajos*.

When nothing remained but the crumbs of a loaf of bread the size and shape of an auto tire, and the neatly picked bones of the stewed fowl strewn about the *skafidi,* we sauntered over to Zarka's *tsera.* It was a tent capable of holding some twenty men seated in a circle, and was nearly full. The attraction was the roast *baloró,* suckling pig, a twenty-five pound turkey, already reduced to mere framework, some flat, flaky cakes that were half bread, half pastry, a bottle of brandy, and several *galone loli mol* (gallons of red wine). It was Zarka's *slavav* (his annual feast day), and the celebration had been going on for two days and nights, during which he had not slept a wink.

Unlike the other men, Zarka worked, himself, selling on street corners from the back of his large Pierce Arrow a patent medicine that he bought from a Chicago drug firm and resold for a profit of 500 per cent. To draw a crowd he would sing, or play a phonograph which he carried about, or make humorous speeches in a flow of funny English. He had the best natural baritone I have ever heard among the gypsies—including some of the Romani singers from famous Moscow choruses who sang recently in Paris—but, being accustomed to improvising on gypsy themes, he had little use for precision of pitch, and his rendering of the American jazz songs he had heard was original, to say the least.

In the center of the *skafidi,* beside the turkey carcass and the browned pig, was a church taper as thick as the calf of your leg. It was carved and painted with gilt, red, and blue designs. It had been burning for forty-eight hours, but was still half as high as the tent pole. To hold it firm it had been set in a silver champagne cooler—filled with chicken feed.

The wine, which had been brought by auto from an Italian grocery, was unusually good for a post-prohibition beverage, a little young, but smacking of the grape, and a trifle effervescent, like many of the semi-sparkling wines of sun-drenched Italy. I have known better wines, but I have never known any to produce more merriment and song.

As it circulated in the one glass, or flowed directly from the gallon jar with a gay glug-glug into some receptive throat, unable to await its turn, it released a corresponding quantity of pent-up joy. Miloš gathered together a chorus of women, who stood in a row in front of the tent and entoned song after song in Romani. The men, seated Turkish fashion within, swayed from side to side or clapped their hands with the rhythm, or joined in the singing, giving shouts of encouragement from time to time.

When the leader of the chorus started a dance song everyone took up the refrain, while one after another of the children, beginning with the oldest girls and ending with a tiny boy barely three, did a gypsy *kelope,* half Oriental, half Russian.

> *"Eh da-le da-le da!*
> *Eh da-le da-le da!"*

Even Miloš, who was nearly eighty and troubled with rheumatism, rose with difficulty from the ground and did a few rapid steps that left him panting, and left the crowd aglow with laughter and enthusiasm.

The last of all to dance was Pitchirika, a pretty girl of seventeen, a Mačvanka, who had recently married into the Kalderaš tribe. Previously she had not struck me as being very beautiful, but as she danced her features were illumined with a flame of pleasure. Her eyes transfixed in turn each pair of eyes that clung to her movements, her expression, and the hidden fire within her that was calling to them. Her hands would be now on her hips as she stamped her feet and swayed the hem of her skirt in a motion like the crest of a wave; now her hands would be raised above her head or along her body in a fluttering, caressing gesture; now they would be out-stretched from the waist, palms upward, the fingers beckoning, beckoning toward her supple body, as she smiled voluptuously and darted a look of soft enticement that all but made each gypsy leap from the ground. She danced with her feet, her body, her hands, but most of all with her smiling lips and her eyes.

Zarka, who was over six feet, good-looking, and vain about his appearance and talents, was the only one who remained unstirred with a sort of mad delight. He was a bit piqued. Swallow-ing a glass of foaming wine at one gulp, he pre-pared to outdo Pitchirika. First he sang a Serbian song in a low voice without much expres-sion. He was merely tuning up. "Sing 'O Čiriklo P'enel' ['The Bird Sings']," pleaded sev-eral in the group. Zarka had apparently aimed to be coaxed to sing this very song, the jewel of his collection, for after beaming gratefully for a moment at the coaxers he began it in a rich warm baritone.

The Romani words flowed together like the clear waters of a brook, making it difficult to separate them and seize the meaning; but I caught enough of them to understand the song. Besides, he sang it so dramatically, so vividly, that it seemed as though one could have followed the thought in a wholly unknown tongue. The idea resembled the fable of "The Town Mouse and the Country Mouse"; but it was about a tame canary and a wild bird. The canary, longing for company, vaunted the advantages of its pretty cage: no hunters, no necessity of providing its own food, no birds of prey; but after listening to each argument the wild bird would reply with the refrain:

"'Tis better in the woods . . ."

Blending their voices with his, men and women, young and old, bass, contralto, and soprano sang the chorus with Zarka:

"*Ciriklo leski p'enel,*
'*Mai feder ando ves . . .'*"

It told of the joy of mating, the joy of greeting the sunlight from aloft, and chief of all the joy of flying hither and thither in the green forest as fancy willed.

There was a certain plaintive sweetness, a certain longing, and heartfelt thankfulness in the expression of the Romanies as they sang. It was as though they were voicing their own unquenchable nostalgia, their gratitude at being delivered from a winter in the cities, and their own joy in the never-ending trail. Zarka had outdone the dancer.

I thought of this a month later when in St. Ouen near Paris a member of a tribe of Nomad gypsy coppersmiths who had returned from China and Japan two years before, and who was getting restless, asked me, as though to try me out, "Why do you go back and forth so much from one country to another?"

"*Romani buči* [Gypsy business]."

"*Čečes,*" she replied, "*Amen sar čiriklé*" ("It's true. We're like the birds").

It was dark before the crowd in the tent began to thin. The fun was getting a bit wild as the new wine went to their heads. "Brother," said Miloš, "if I were you I would leave the *Romen kai matsioven* [the gypsies to get drunk]. Sometimes they don't know what they're doing. If they started a quarrel and hurt you, they'd cut off a finger the next day; but that wouldn't help you, would it?" I noticed that nearly a third of the men who stayed had scars from knife wounds on their faces, and prudently I followed the example of Miloš, who went to his tent to sleep.

I spread the *šeran* and lay for a while propped on one elbow, looking out of the open fly. In front of a number of tents the coals from the supper fires were still smoldering, a dull red glow. In other tents lanterns were burning, making them gleam like huge red and yellow lamp shades. From Zarka's *tsera* came a long oblong of light projected on the grass of the clearing, a nightmare of weird distorted shadows on the patch of light, and along the canvas walls, sounds of brief quarreling, loud laughter, snatches of song, until finally the noise of the *slava* ceased.

Other tents were invisible in the darkness. The rounded tops of the oak trees and the sharp silhouette of an occasional pine tree stood out against the deep transparent sky, blending a star or two with the foliage like tiny candles on a Christmas tree.

The whippoorwill no longer called to its mate. Silence settled on the camp and the woods, soft as dust. I tried to keep awake to gaze at the stars, but the stillness and the peace gently closed my eyes. . . .

Late the following afternoon a sheriff and two deputies appeared in a Ford and put an end to the camp at Thornton. "I gave yez till Saturday night to pack up and get out uv here, yuh pack of damn bums! Now if yuh don't git in an hour, I'll make you *git,* if I have to come back with half the county and a bunch of shotguns!" Woršo was a model of patience and Christian humility. He quietly stated that one of the children was ill, which happened to be true; but it made no difference. Seeing the sheriff meant business this time, Woršo gave the order to strike tents. Within an hour everything was loaded into autos and the caravan was on its way.

The sick boy was taken back to Chicago, where the parents had already spent several thousand dollars consulting the best specialists, the clinics, and numerous quacks. For a week they had lain on the floor beside his bed in the hospital, breaking all rules and driving nurses, internes, and doctors half distracted.

The rest of the band divided, part going west, part going in the direction of Hammond, Indiana. Liubo le Miloške, in whose machine I was riding, went with the latter. I was glad to be on the road again, though still incensed at the sheriff. My companions, however, felt no anger. Eviction was merely an ordinary incident, one of the commonest occurrences in their lives and the lives of their ancestors for numberless generations. It was fate; and fate is better met with a jest than with a frown.

The joy of being on the gypsy trail again was all the greater for me because of the many difficulties I had encountered in my way. I had imagined that it would be easy for me to "join the gypsies," with my many friends among the nomads; but I should have known better. Their peculiar patriarchal organization makes an unattached male unnecessary and unwanted. One can really join such a tribe only by marriage; and it was the idea that doubtless I would soon do so and would make a worthy *Rom*—the word meaning both gypsy and husband—for some *bori,* some marriageable girl, that made them accept me as a temporary member.

My first disappointment was in Cincinnati. About the time I was ready to "join them," I read in the newspaper that a series of petty crimes had been committed by gypsies from two large bands and that some of them had been arrested. I went to the police station and learned that they were out on bail, but not even the detectives knew where I could find them. I went to the usual camping grounds, only to learn that they had suddenly departed. Forfeiture of bail was preferable to even a week or two in jail.

> *"Ciriklo p'enel leski,*
> *Mai feder ando ves . . .' "*

At any rate, I knew I should find gypsies in Chicago. A month previously, while in that city I had trailed some Romani children to a doorway above a store on the West Side.

"O dat khere?" ("Is your father home?") I asked.

"Ei [yes]," the oldest boy answered, his eyes wide with wonder at a *Gajo*-looking person addressing him in *Romanes.* From the hallway of the top floor I heard a violent storm of argument, yelling of children, and a cursing of parents to quiet them, that means a certain variety of gypsy

dwelling. I pushed open the door and saw some twenty individuals squatting on the floor of what had once been a shady café. The place was filthy. Rags littered the floor. There was a neat round hole in the dirty plate-glass window where someone had thrown a stone. The lower part was masked by heavy hangings of gaudy India print, which must have excluded most of the light by day. A single dim lamp lighted the room by night. The hole alone admitted fresh air.

Four families lived in the one room. Some were quarreling, others eating. A woman was delousing her small daughter. I shook hands with the men and squatted on the floor. They were Greek and Turkish gypsies, *XorXane* and *Balame Roma*. A boy entered with a platter of roasted sheeps' heads, the white skulls shining through the patches of browned flesh, the teeth grinning sardonically, the sunken eye sockets staring lugubriously. They were evidently regarded as a great treat. *"Le, prala, le!"* ("Take some, brother, take some!"), said the gypsy who had sent for them.

"Nai bokhalo" ("I'm not hungry"), I answered. *"Nais tuke"* ("Thank you.")

"Pes rakia?" ("Will you have some liquor?") What gypsy ever could honestly say that he was not thirsty? I was therefore forced to accept. My host, Todor, brought from a corner a five-

gallon wicker-covered glass container such as acids are shipped in, and poured out a glass of moonshine. I noticed that the container was nearly empty, and, seeing that no one had been blinded by drinking the stuff, and surmising that no one had been killed by it, I cautiously sipped some. It was slow torture. An aged grandmother who was scarcely able to walk begged for a little of it. Todor motioned to me to finish mine so that he could give her the glass. A moment later the woman began to screech and howl.. What! Another case of prohibition poisoning, I wonder? Unconsciously my hand sought the pit of my stomach. No. The trouble was merely caused by a group of kids, who were laughing in a corner. They had stolen Grandma's whisky.

When I got up to go I asked my host, *"Savo Todor san tu?"* (Which Todor are you?") "There are so many Todors. I want to know, because if I meet any of our people they will ask me whom I saw in Chicago."

"Tell them, *'Todor kai marde le Romea'* ['Todor-who-murdered-the-gypsies']. They all know me by that name." I learned later that he had killed his father-in-law and several others in a moment of rage.

On my return to Chicago the last time in quest of gypsies with whom to take the road, I found their usual haunts deserted. In desperation I looked for Todor-who-killed-the-gypsies, but even he was gone. Perhaps the police have chased them all out, I thought; and my hopes fell.

At last, however, I found an old acquaintance, Dušan le Peroske, a Romani who had lost one eye in a revolver battle. His wife was standing in a doorway beside a phrenology sign, "We read your head like you read open book." She greeted me cordially and told me that Dušan was not at home; but to go upstairs and wait while she sent a boy for him. At the head of the stairs I saw a grinning girl of nine or ten peeking from behind a pile of bedding. I went into the one living room and waited. It happened that the girl had been going about naked, and had sought the nearest refuge on my approach. Unfortunately, her one dress was in the room where I was waiting. After some ten minutes of being marooned in the hallway, she gathered courage to steal slyly into the room, snatch a dress off a nail, and slip it on. But, alas, it was her little sister's and only reached her waist. Her sense of modesty, however, had been satisfied.

The last time I had seen Dušan he was singing drunk and exceedingly friendly. He had offered me his twenty-four-year-old daughter as a bride for nothing. To be sure, she was a widow and had two children, but she was not bad-looking and was a good fortune teller—an excellent breadwinner. He had shown me her picture dressed in all her brilliant finery. I had attributed his generosity to wine, but wrongly. The moment he returned he gently reproached me for not having come back to Chicago sooner and accepted his offer. *"Či mangav love—numai čačimus"* ["I don't want money—only truth"], he said. "Lots of American gypsies want to marry her, but she doesn't want them, and I wouldn't let her if she did. The boys born in this country are only after money. They're like the *Gajos*. They're not worth *ek ful*. They go with *raklva*. What's money compared with my daughter's happiness?"

"But she has never seen me and I have only seen her picture," I said.

"No matter. If you want her I'll send a telegram to Youngstown and have her come here," he answered. I begged him not to bother; but without saying anything more about it, he actually sent the telegram a day or two later.

In the meantime he took me to a Greek café where some fifteen Romanies were drinking "good beer," with four or five odd per cent of alcoholic content. They had been here since ten in the morning and remained until six that night. When we entered they were fairly hilarious. Stivo, whose father was away at the time, was exulting in his temporary chieftainship. He and Zarka, who secretly coveted the leadership, were having a contest to see who could spend the most money. The beers cost *ek franco* (a quarter each), which facilitated their ambitions. Stivo ordered three times as many glasses as there were men, and, as the last round had not been finished, he shouted, "You're not ready yet," and swept the whole line of glasses off the bar with a blow of his arm.

Two thick-set, red-faced detectives in plain clothes entered and drank some whisky. "Hello! There's Steve's gang," said one of them. Three of the gypsies bought drinks for them, knowing their good will might be useful some day. As one of them clinked glass with a gypsy he proposed a whisky toast:

> " 'To the lips and past the gums—
> Look out guts! Here she comes!' "

The gypsy bought them another drink, and offered a toast in Romani. From the benevolent smile which he gave as he looked the detective squarely in the eye, the officer thought it must be something extremely complimentary, for he beamed in return. As a matter of fact, it was, *"Xa mro khar!"* the deadliest of insults.

About six o'clock an auto truck drove up to the café with a strange load. It was filled with some twenty Romani girls who had been collected at various fortune-telling booths about the city by a gypsy boy who was to deliver them to their husbands and fathers at the camps outside the city. They were chatting and laughing with glee at the prospect of escaping from work and city and of being back in the green country again. Their dresses formed a hundred different color ·combinations, and a gayer, livelier, more brilliant picture would be inconceivable. I envied them.

I consulted Dušan about going out to the camp at Thornton, but he discouraged me. After two days in town, however, I took the train for Thornton alone, and walked out to the camp. It was so well hidden that I would never have discovered it if an English gypsy girl, a Smith, who was weaving baskets beside a tent on the highway, had not told me where to find it. The attempt to "join them" was unavailing. My reception was cold. After they had satisfied their curiosity they left me to my own resources. Disappointed, I started homeward. An auto full of gypsy men passed me and stopped. As though sorry for not having been more hospitable, they offered to drive me back to Chicago.

One of them, Big Milano, explained that my only hope of camping and traveling with them was through marriage into the tribe. "Have you a car?" he asked. I answered that I was going to wait until I got a wife. "Get a car first," he advised, "and you'll find it easier to get a wife." He added that it would be useful for chicken stealing.

Another gypsy told me of a camp on Archer Avenue, just outside of Chicago, where I should find a gypsy named Filipo with a widowed daughter. "You can get her cheap," he said. "She wants to marry some one who can drive her car for her."

As I could not even drive an auto, another solution of my problem was necessary. "I know," said a third. "You say you haven't got much money. I know how you can get a wife for nothing. Tsino has two wives and they fight all the time. He wants to get rid of the youngest. You go to him and tell him you want his wife." I had seen Tsino in the café, and a fierce-looking pirate he was.

"Can you see me going to a *Rom* I hardly know and asking him for his wife?" I said. They laughed and Milano replied, "Tell him I sent you, *O Baro Milano.*"

"No. I'm afraid."

"*Mišto,* very well, I'll take you there now. I was going near his *ófisa.*"

What was I to do? Supposing Tsino offered me one of his wives, glad to get rid of her, and should be offended if I refused? Happily, at that moment we passed a house where some other gypsies were living, and I made an excuse that I wanted to get out and see them.

The next day I went to a camp of Rumanian gypsies on the edge of a suburb, but I found them

too tame. The Nomads call them *Baiáš,* and,
although the older women dress not unlike the
Nomads, they are very different. They speak
no Romani save what they have picked up from
traveling with the Anglo-American gypsies, the
only ones with whom they associate much. On
another occasion I should have been delighted at
the find; but my heart was set on traveling with
the Nomads. I was ready to do anything—except marry one.

On my return to Chicago that day, I heard
good news—Woršo, the chief, whom I knew well,
had come back. Through his intercession I was
granted my wish. I bought a tent at an army
store; Woršo lent me a huge eiderdown *šeran*
for a bed—it was summer, and he had more than
he needed—and Liubo let me travel in his auto,
as long as I paid for the gasoline (*o gazo*).

It was all as pleasant as I had expected. Wandering through the countryside in June and
pitching our tents wherever we came to a good
spot was happiness. But the constant idling, the
dulce far niente all day in camp, finally became
a bit too dulcet. One must be born on the road
to learn the gentle art of doing nothing from
morning till night.

We circled back, and made camp the following
week near Blue Island. There I learned that
Dušan's widowed daughter had arrived in
Chicago and they were expecting to join us, that

Tsino and his two wives were also coming, and that the *diwano* was to be held the next day. Nura was sure to be freed and Ili would keep urging me to marry her. In addition, Woršo had picked a bride for me. That night I was to go with him in the traditional manner with a gallon of whisky and make the necessary overtures to her father. If he liked me, all would be settled. The matrimonial plot was getting too thick.

I asked Liubo to take me to town, where I managed to lose him. Then I sent a telegram to Woršo, care of a roadhouse near the camp: "Called away on business. You can have my tent."

Ten days later in New York I was homesick for my gypsies. I hunted in vain through lower Manhattan, Sheepshead Bay, and Coney Island in their old haunts. At Coney a clerk in a cigar store informed me that one of them had stolen a gold watch from a man whose fortune she was telling. Woe the day! The man was a detective! To be able to unlock the secrets of the future, and not be able to spot a bull a block away—what a paradox! I knew all further search would be vain.

However, there was one consolation: in a few days I should be on the ocean, where even *Gajos* can enjoy the sweet-do-nothing, where life is as informal as a gypsy camp, where one can drink in nature to the fullest. For a year I should be free to wander wherever I wished: to see my old Gitano friends in Spain, to hear the gypsy fiddles cry once more in Budapest, to hear the Russian Romanies in Paris sing their intoxicating songs. Perhaps I should hear once more the refrain of the wild bird who refused the comforts of a cage, telling his tame brother how good it is in the woods, how good it is to be free.

I shall be back once more on the never-ending trail.

THE END.